W9-BZB-447

INSIDE BUCKINGHAM PALACE

ANDREW MORTON

SUMMIT BOOKS

New York London Toronto Sydney Tokyo

In Memory of Mary Anne Sanders

ACKNOWLEDGEMENTS

The story of life inside Buckingham Palace has been immeasurably
enhanced by the anecdotes, insights and assistance of Margaret Carter, Lucinda
Craig Harvey, Roger Courtier, Geoffrey Dickens MP, Jeff Edwards, Michael
Fagan, Alan Hamilton, Paul Henderson, Neil Mackwood, James Mooney Boyle,
Michael Nash, Phyllis Pearsall, Joy Pinder, James Rusbridger and Judy Wade.
My thanks also to those who work or have worked at Buckingham Palace,
the Foreign Office and the Metropolitan Police. Their background
guidance and information has helped give a fresh perspective on the
palace world. As ever my publisher Michael O'Mara has been
the source of sage advice and enthusiasm while my wife
Lynne has been a tireless supporter.

Andrew Morton
March 1991

PICTURE ACKNOWLEDGEMENTS

The Publishers would like to thank the following sources:
Alpha: 8, 21, 34, 44, 51, 52, 63, 71, 75, 87, 90; Camera Press: 5, 14, 15,
(top and botom) 20, 30, (top and bottom) 31, (top), 32, 35, 37, 45 (top right and bottom),
64, 81, 92; Tim Graham: 3, 9, 18, 22, 29, 31 (bottom), 39, 47, 48, 49, 58, 72 (main picture and
top left), 77, 78, 86, 93; Glen Harvey: 6, 7, 8, 23, 25, 38, 41, 55, 59, 76, 94 (top and bottom), 95
(bottom); Reproduced by Gracious Permission of Her Majesty the Queen: 2, 12, 13, 26, 27 (top and
bottom), 50, 56, 61, 67, 70, 84, 85; Hulton-Deutch: 19, 45; Anwar Hussein: 42, 65, 67
(bottom left), 69, 80; National Portrait Gallery, London: 9; Nunn Syndication: 16,
33, 40, 62, 66; Photographers International: 1, 16, 17, 46, 72, 82, 88, 89, 91;
Popperfoto: 19 (middle and bottom left); Rex Features: 11, 83;
Syndication International: 79.

SUMMIT BOOKS
Simon & Schuster Building
Rockefeller Center
1230 Avenue of the Americas
New York, New York 10020

Text copyright © 1991 by Andrew Morton

All rights reserved including the right of reproduction in whole or in part in any form

Originally published in Great Britain by Michael O'Mara Books Limited, London

Quality printing and binding in Hong Kong by Mandarin Offset

10 9 8 7 6 5 4 3 2 1

Library of Congress cataloging and publication data available on request

ISBN 0-671-74961-7

Typeset by Florencetype Ltd, Kewstoke, Avon

CONTENTS

I   THE HOUSE   7

II   AT HOME WITH THE ROYAL FAMILY   33

III   UPSTAIRS DOWNSTAIRS   49

IV   BY ROYAL COMMAND   63

V   PANIC AT THE PALACE   77

VI   POMP ON PARADE   89

Appendix – the cost of running Buckingham Palace   96

I

THE HOUSE

*T*he winter snow fell ceaselessly, clothing Buckingham Palace in an uncharacteristic white garb and blanketing the nation's capital, which quickly collapsed into chaos.

In her first-floor study, the Queen paused from the blizzard of paperwork on her desk and looked outside her window, the fierce snow flurries blurring the traffic as it crawled along Constitution Hill. Setting aside the serious purpose of her state papers, the Queen was seized by a simple sentimental impulse. She decided to feed the ducks standing shivering beside the palace lake.

That kindly gesture sent a small army into action. First the Queen rang the silver bell on her desk which summoned her most senior servant, the Page of the Back Stairs. Ever alert to that familiar tinkle, Christopher Bray stopped his work, adjusted his blue tailcoat and black tie, and hurried from his vestibule across the corridor from the Queen's study into the royal presence.

Once informed of the monarch's wish, Bray set well-oiled machinery in motion. He passed the message to the 'number one' footman who telephoned the chef in the palace kitchens. While the kitchen staff busied themselves cutting bread into

The raising of the Sovereign's standard traditionally shows that the Queen is in residence. It is a home with no number on the door but the coat of arms on the gates reveals the identity of its residents.

uniform strips, another footman in his distinctive scarlet waistcoat made the half-mile round trip to pick up the carefully wrapped package.

During this scurry of activity, the Queen's senior dresser Peggy Hoath was busy in the regal dressing room which adjoins the study. For once there was no need to leaf through the leather-bound wardrobe books that record every last detail of regal attire. From memory, Peggy picked out the Sovereign's favourite green herringbone overcoat, galoshes, gloves and woollen scarf. Then she carefully laid out this royal attire as her mistress prepared to brave the winter chill.

The Queen's page himself attended to the most important accessory in the monarch's life, her corgis. Christopher summoned Fable, Myth, Spark and the rest of the royal pack from their cosy quarters which are located conveniently near to the study. Finally he delivered the packet of bread, naturally on a solid-silver salver, to await the Queen's pleasure.

So, on a leaden day in February 1991, the assorted ducks, swans, geese and pink flamingos were treated to the Queen's largesse in an episode which perfectly illustrates the fascination of Buckingham Palace. It is the constant contrast between commonplace domesticity and the gilded setting which gives the palace its special appeal.

This natural curiosity to see just how the other half lives is recognized by the royal family. As the

Duke of Edinburgh observes, 'What happens on the other side of a wall is always an intriguing question and when the wall is in the middle of London and encloses the garden of Buckingham Palace it is positively tantalizing.'

The contrasts between the remote regal image and domestic reality are endless. In the kitchens for example there are long typed lists pinned to the wall referring to the mealtime preferences of the latest infant occupants of the second-floor nursery, Princesses Eugenie and Beatrice. The formality of stating that 'Their Royal Highnesses' should be served Rice Krispies and Cornflakes for breakfast, hot milk at supper and 'on no account be given pork sausages' is amusingly incongruous.

Wander into the Queen's study in the evening and you may see the Head of State, her glasses perched on the end of her nose, a glass of white German Spätlese wine by her side, poring over *The Times* crossword. It takes her just four minutes – she has been timed.

The feeling is rather like being allowed back-

The Queen's corgis are constantly by her side. They even have their own bedroom near to her study.

Princess Diana, her hair still wet from her morning swim in the pool, returns to Kensington Palace.

stage during Shakespeare's *King Lear* and seeing the tragic monarch, a cigarette in one hand and a glass of beer in the other, making idle chitchat. While the experience does not shatter the illusion, it gives you a different perspective on the drama.

Long-serving staff are still taken aback when they see Princess Diana, her hair wet from her morning swim in the palace pool, wandering along the corridor, or Princess Anne, dressed in her tiara and full evening regalia, hurrying for an appointment with an artist first thing in the morning.

Two media executives chortle over the day they were leaving the palace office of Prince Charles's former private secretary Sir John Riddel and were introduced to a young man wearing jeans, sweatshirt and training shoes. One media mogul chatted to the young man while Sir John looked on, smiling. After they had said their goodbyes the dynamic duo walked to their car. 'Who was the kid?' asked the silent one. His colleague looked at him in

ing

amazement: 'That was Prince Andrew.'

It soon becomes clear that while we may regard Buckingham Palace as a combination of museum and office block, for the royal family its majestic rooms, endless corridors and 39 acres of manicured garden are home. They talk of activities in The Mall in the same way that we discuss events in our own street. So the Duchess of York tells her friends about the day the palace police stopped the traffic so a mother duck from the palace lake could take her brood of chicks to St James's Park; and over lunch the Queen may inform Princess Diana that she saw the Olympic gold medallist Steve Ovett training in Hyde Park, while Prince Philip rails against the taxi-drivers who won't give way when he is trying to drive his electric-powered Lucas van out of the palace gates.

Indeed the human scale of such a grandiose mansion disconcerts those unwary visitors who are steeling themselves for a stiff royal encounter.

Princess Anne's hairdresser Michael Rasser had the wind taken out of his sails when he was rugby-

Prince Andrew, who wanders round the palace in casual clothes, often goes unrecognized by visitors.

Royal duties include posing for official paintings. Here Princess Anne stands for the artist John Ward.

tackled by a hearty Prince Andrew as he was waiting to attend to his royal client. On another occasion a Lady Clerk, as the secretaries are known, was astonished to see the Queen running pell-mell along the Household Corridor in hot pursuit of Prince William. 'Don't worry, this will happen to you one day,' she said breathlessly when she noticed the young woman smiling at the scene. Fifty years previously it was the infant Princess Elizabeth who surprised the starchy Archbishop of Canterbury Cosmo Lang when he saw her leading George V round his study floor by his grey beard.

Equally mysterious for the palace inmates is life beyond the gravelled courtyard. When she was a child the Queen, then Princess Elizabeth, spent hours looking out of the window of the Yellow Drawing Room, watching the cars and the people. She says, 'I used to wonder what they were doing and where they were all going, and what they thought about outside the palace.'

BUCKINGHAM PALACE
PLANS OF THE PRINCIPAL AND BEDROOM FLOORS

PRINCIPAL FLOOR

① THE BLUE AND YELLOW SUITE
② THE CENTRE ROOM
③ THE BUHL GUEST SUITE
④ THE CHINESE DINING ROOM
⑤ JUNK ROOM
⑥ PRINCE PHILIP'S SUITE
⑦ THE QUEEN'S BEDROOM SUITE
⑧ THE QUEEN'S STUDY
⑨ PAGE'S VESTIBULE
⑩ CORGI'S BEDROOM
⑪ THE QUEEN'S DINING ROOM
⑫ GIFT ROOM
⑬ THE AUDIENCE CHAMBER
⑭ THE MALL

BEDROOM FLOOR

① EQUERRY'S BEDROOM
② LADY-IN-WAITING'S SUITE
③ THE DUKE AND DUCHESS OF YORK'S SUITE
④ PRINCESS ANNE'S SUITE
⑤ THE NURSERY
⑥ THE NURSERY LIFT
⑦ PRINCE EDWARD'S SUITE
⑧ THE QUEEN'S WARDROBE
⑨ BOBO MACDONALD'S SUITE
⑩ LIFT

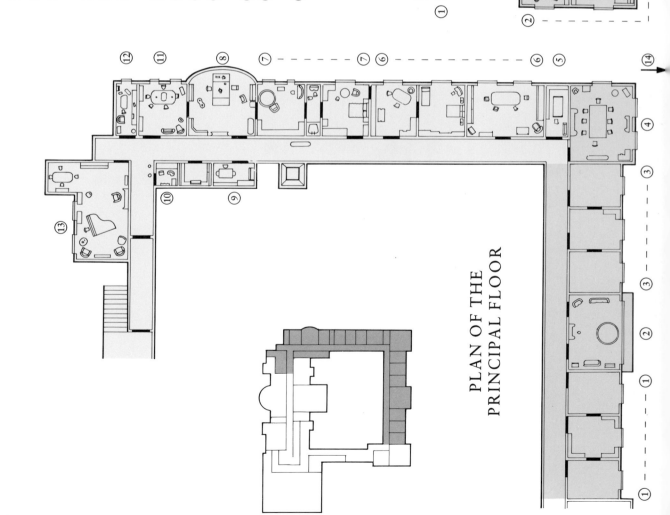

PLAN OF THE PRINCIPAL FLOOR

PLAN OF THE BEDROOM FLOOR

She has managed to escape the remorseless royal script only a few times in her life, most memorably on VE night when thousands gathered outside the palace to cheer the royal family as the nation celebrated the ending of the Second World War. Princess Elizabeth and Princess Margaret slipped out of a side door and mingled unnoticed with the milling throng.

They had experienced the sensation of standing on the balcony waving to the people; now they wanted to view life from the other side of the green baize door. The Queen told broadcaster Godfrey Talbot, 'My parents went outside on to the balcony in response to the huge crowds outside. Then when the excitement of the floodlights being switched on got through to us, all of a sudden I

The palace occupies a small geographical area but exerts an influence far beyond its borders.

realized I couldn't see what the crowds were enjoying.'

Those few stolen hours bring back vivid memories. 'I remember lines of unknown people linking arms and walking down Whitehall and we were all swept along by tides of happiness and relief.'

Wondering what life is like in the 'real world' is a common royal experience. During Princess Diana's stay at the palace before her marriage, she watched the world outside the palace, possibly regretting that she would never again be able to slip into a life of cosy anonymity. Prince Andrew enjoys telling visitors to his second-floor apartment that he dare not pull back the net curtains because tourists start waving. 'I should put a dummy of myself in the window,' he jokes.

The Duchess of York, the newest arrival to the palace, describes her new home as 'the best hotel in London' and enjoys inviting her friends for after-

noon tea or late-night supper parties. Prince Charles, who was born in the first-floor Buhl Room, refers to Buckingham Palace in the time-honoured way. In memos to staff and letters to friends he calls his former home 'the House'. Indeed the royal family are so used to calling it the House that when Prince Edward worked for the Really Useful Theatre Company at the Palace Theatre he could not understand why his colleagues burst into fits of laughter each time he answered the phone with the greeting, 'Hello, it's Edward from the Palace.'

The House has been the London residence of every generation of the royal family since Queen Victoria's time and is currently the home of the Queen, the Duke of Edinburgh, Princess Anne and Prince Edward as well as the Duke and Duchess of

The Centre Room ABOVE is where the royal family gathers before appearing on the balcony. The Green Drawing Room RIGHT has mirrored doors to give an effect of light, space and magnificence.

York and their children, Princesses Beatrice and Eugenie.

The world's most prestigious address had humble beginnings. James I first used the site in an ill-fated scheme to cultivate mulberry trees for silkworms to feed on. Then the gardens degenerated into an open-air brothel which, according to the diarist Samuel Pepys, attracted a 'rascally, whoring, roguing sort of people'. The Duke of Buckingham built Buckingham House in 1703 but the site, commanding an enviable prospect of The Mall, incited royal jealousy: in 1762 George III

During her reign the Queen Mother (here seen with her grandchildren) helped replant the garden.

managed to buy the property for the princely sum of £28,000.

Though George III brought the building into royal possession it was his son George IV who was responsible for an imaginative rebuilding programme under the inspiration of the architect John Nash. The transformation took a thousand men, often working by candlelight until ten o'clock at night. However, progress was so slow that the King never lived in the palace, and his brother and successor William IV so loathed the palace that he tried to foist it on to the army for use as a barracks.

On 13 July 1837 the palace, which was by then seen as an expensive white elephant, started its royal life proper when Queen Victoria became the first sovereign to make it her official residence. At that time the royal home was built round only three sides of the central courtyard and when Queen Victoria drove to her coronation at Westminster Abbey her state coach passed under Marble Arch, which stood in front of the palace.

In 1847 the Marble Arch was moved to its present site in Hyde Park Corner, where it is now marooned as a glorified traffic island, so that Edward Blore could properly design the new east front of the palace. This is the sombre face of stolid respectability the world now sees. This frowning frontage, subsequently dressed in cold, solemn Portland stone, is symbolic of the change in Queen Victoria's character following the death of her beloved consort Prince Albert.

In the early days of her reign the grace and sunny splendour of the original palace was matched by royal life. The rooms echoed to the sound of the court orchestra, regular Monday dances and the chatter of the 'respectable classes' at formal receptions. The Queen took her children sledging in the gardens and loved showing visitors around the palace.

When Albert died of typhoid it was as though the clocks stopped. The palace became a claustrophobic mausoleum dedicated to his memory. Indeed his rooms were left exactly as they were on the day he died in December 1861. Albert's walking sticks, his despatch boxes, his paperweights, even his medicine glass were all preserved. In a macabre ceremony a servant filled his washbasin with water each evening. The queen stayed at Buckingham Palace so rarely – only eight nights a year – that one wag hung a For Sale sign on the gates.

It is little wonder that Edward VII described the palace as a 'sepulchre'. One of his first actions on becoming king was to march through the funereal rooms sweeping away hated memories of his youth. He broke busts of the Queen's faithful retainer John Brown with his cane and cleared out roomfuls of yellowing elephant tusks and other useless memorabilia.

In the next reign, Queen Mary capitalized on the improvements set in train by Edward VII and was reluctant to leave when Edward VIII became king. 'Those lovely comfortable rooms which have been my happy home,' Queen Mary said when, with some regret, she moved to Marlborough House.

Her reluctance is understandable. For it was Queen Mary's energy and enterprise which were responsible for restoring the state apartments to their former glory. As a lover of the Regency period she scoured other royal residences and antique shops tracking down furniture and *objets d'art* relating to the age of George IV. She rummaged through the palace storerooms unearthing treasures which had been despised and forgotten.

Not everyone is impressed by this mirrored and marbled splendour. 'This was a palace in the grand style,' reflected the Live Aid organizer Bob Geldof when he arrived for a Handel concert. 'Perhaps the private rooms are cosy, but the reception rooms seemed garish and too brightly lit. The gold leaf was too gold, the white paint too white, the Chinese vases were placed without an eye for proportion. I was disappointed.'

His views are shared by royalty. Edward VIII was a reluctant tenant of what the Duke of Edinburgh calls 'a tied cottage', observing that the lighting in the state rooms made the women look 'ghastly'. Yet he hesitated to make the kind of improvements Wallis Simpson had in mind; 'One day all this will be tennis courts,' she said as she looked over the lawns. Years later Edward gave his reasons. 'One never tinkers with palaces: like museums they seem to resist change,' he wrote. 'This vast building with its stately rooms and endless corridors and passages . . . seemed pervaded by a curious, musty smell that still assails me whenever I enter its portals. I was never happy there.'

The Duchess of York is the latest royal resident and describes the palace as 'the best hotel in London'.

Princess Anne was born and bred in the palace, but now spends most of her time at her country home.

While George VI complained the place was an 'icebox', his children saw the palace as a huge playground. Princess Elizabeth's first impression was practical. 'People here need bicycles,' she observed and gazed with horrified fascination at the work of the full-time 'vermin man'. One of her favourite games was to walk to and fro past the soldiers. Her royal status meant that each time she walked by they had to present arms. Her younger sister Princess Margaret relished the move from 145 Piccadilly to the most illustrious address in the land. She rode along the corridors on her tricycle, followed the palace clock-winder on his rounds and startled visitors by jumping from behind pillars into their path.

'It was if the place had been dead for years and had suddenly come alive,' said one member of staff. Since then it has been the royal children who have helped turn the House into a lively home which gives a human scale to sober state ceremonial. It may be a palace in the grand tradition but there is a child's pedal-car at the Garden Entrance and Princess Eugenie's baby buggy is regularly wheeled along the red-carpeted corridors, past the displays of delicate porcelain and the huge gilt-framed portraits of long-dead ancestors and heroic naval battles.

However Buckingham Palace is not the place to go to see a washing line in the back garden. Domestic it may be; casual it is not. When writer Anthony Sampson dissected British society in *The New Anatomy of Britain* he observed that 'the view from the palace is like looking at Britain from backstage, where sets, floodlights and props are seen as part of the illusion'. This image is ultimately misleading. For even without the make-up and costumes, there is still a formality between members of the royal family as the drama continues behind closed doors.

In February 1991 for example Prince Edward wished to see his father to discuss the theatrical

RIGHT The notice on the palace gates announces the birth of Prince William. BELOW Prince Harry enjoys a ride after the Queen's birthday parade.

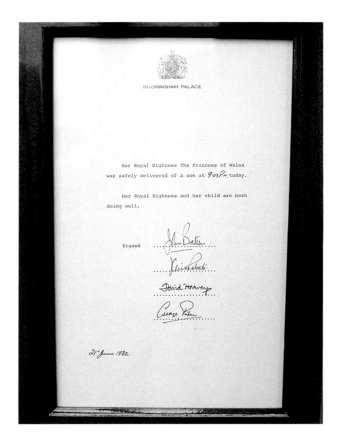

venture he had started with three colleagues. There was no question of his simply dropping into the Duke of Edinburgh's private apartments for a chat. The Prince, who lives on the floor above his father, first asked his valet to make an appointment with the Duke's valet to see if the Duke was free for dinner. He greeted his father with a brief neck bow and in turn the Duke kissed his son on the forehead – a traditional greeting between royal princes when they meet in private.

However Edward, who had entertained his girlfriend Anastasia Cooke to tea earlier that afternoon, was spared the ordeal of wearing the formal clothes endured by his ancestors. Each time the then Prince of Wales, later Edward VIII, dined with his parents he had to wear the Garter Star on his tailcoat; and a morning coat was required when calling upon his father George V.

While Prince Edward calls the Duke 'Papa', there is no such informality when the Princess of Wales sees the Queen. Both she and the Duchess of York greet the Queen with a kiss on each cheek and on the hand followed by a deep formal curtsy. Thereafter they call her 'Ma'am' – not the family name of 'Lillibet'.

Indeed much of the theatre of modern monarchy is the observance of social niceties, an uneasy marriage of good manners and class distinction. Buckingham Palace is the perfect auditorium for the performance of this ornate drama. Princess Anne's former dresser Linda Joyce observes, 'When she goes out of the door it's like her going on to the stage.'

Props are on hand to assist the central players to make suitably dramatic entrances. At the annual reception for the diplomatic corps – the ambassadors specifically assigned to various state rooms according to their length of service – the Queen, Princess Diana and the rest of the royal family make a spectacular entrance through a fireplace.

The family assembles in the Royal Closet, a little drawing room containing valuable early Italian paintings collected by Prince Albert. At a signal from the Queen a servant touches a spring in an ebony china cabinet and the whole fireplace swings open to the adjoining White Drawing Room, allowing the royal family to make an impressive *coup de théâtre*.

A bored Prince Harry flicks biscuit crumbs as troops below the balcony are reviewed by the Queen.

For a diplomat this intentional sense of occasion begins when ambassadors present their credentials to court. Instead of a limousine, they are conveyed by coach and horses. Inevitably there is a strict hierarchy : high commissioners are assigned four horses, ambassadors only two. Funny things rarely happen on the way to the palace as every detail is catered for. There is even a lady from the Foreign Office who visits the wives of diplomats before the royal audience to teach them how to curtsy. A chair is used as a substitute for the Queen. These theatrical touches have a purpose, helping to create a positive impression among the most influential visitors to Britain.

In the same way, nothing so prosaic as a van is used to deliver the Queen's mail. Every day the Queen's Messenger, driving an immaculate navy brougham, trots around the various government departments, delivering and picking up official messages. However, in these security-conscious times, the famous red boxes containing secret documents for the Queen are sent in a secure government van, a coat of arms painted on its black sides.

Even breakfast has a theatrical flavour, the Queen's Pipe Major playing Scottish airs for fifteen minutes every day under her study while the Sovereign peruses her unironed copy of *The Times*. She rather misses the special royal edition which was printed on high-quality newsprint. The pipe-

The royal family watches attentively as a flypast marks the 50th anniversary of the Battle of Britain.

playing is a custom dating back to Queen Victoria's times, but Prince Philip is said to be indifferent to the skirl of the pipes.

These productions assume Hollywood proportions for state occasions. At banquets the Palace Steward operates a set of traffic lights behind the Queen's chair to direct the heavy traffic of footmen and butlers in order to prevent a pile-up of plates. It took three days to lay the tables for Princess Diana's wedding breakfast and another three days to do the washing up.

The scale of the palace reflects the epic displays it stages. There are around 2,000 locks for the 661 rooms and safes, and about 300 clocks, including one made in 1695, which take Mr Pusey and his colleague a week to wind and service, as well as 2,000 electric light bulbs to be regularly replaced. As palace postmen deliver the 1,500 or so letters to the numerous departments they appreciate the many floral bouquets brightening the rooms and corridors which full-time florists arrange.

With rooms specifically set aside for television and radio broadcasts and used to store everything from ice-cream, china and glassware to the Queen's Christmas gifts, it is not surprising that when Queen Mary first moved in she got lost for three hours as she explored the three miles of corridors and rooms. The maze is so intricate, with hidden doors, tiny cupboards and obscure com-

partments, that the strangest things turn up. A set of carpenter's tools, untouched for 200 years, were found in one corner while a painting by the European master Anthony Van Dyck stood for years in a servants' corridor, neglected and undiscovered. It even bore the water marks of the cleaner's floor mop.

In such a labyrinth it is little wonder that cleaners have in their armoury more than twenty different types of household brush, some specially designed for the palace. There are long-handled brushes to dust the intricate mouldings on the ceilings, and others with small velvet strips tacked round the head to protect the furniture from scratches. Huge walk-in wardrobes are used to preserve the military uniforms of George V and VI which are maintained in pristine condition by a valet, while the basement storerooms are filled with bizarre gifts from a lifetime's travels. How many household cellars boast a collection of shrunken heads? Buckingham Palace has that doubtful distinction.

The most valuable gifts are stored in a converted air-raid shelter deep beneath the palace. Only the Yeoman of the Gold Plate is allowed access to the hydraulic lift which goes down to a veritable Aladdin's cave of unimagined wealth accrued at a time when the sun never set on the British Empire and tribute from its domains – especially India and South Africa – showered on the House of Windsor. There are ruby, emerald and pearl necklaces, diamond-encrusted swords and scabbards,

THE PALACE IN WARTIME

The palace's finest hour was when it was bombed nine times during the Second World War. One daring daylight raid was so accurate – the pilot flying along The Mall after diving from low cloud – that a furious King George VI suspected that it was a German relative who had visited the palace during peacetime and knew the local geography.

As a propaganda ploy Goering's decision to target the palace badly backfired. It meant that for the first time royalty and its subjects were seen to be on equal terms. As George VI recorded in his diary, 'I feel that our tours of bombed areas in London are helping the people who have lost their relations and homes and we have both found a new bond with them as Buckingham Palace has been bombed as well as their homes and nobody is immune.'

Generations later the Queen continued this democratic tradition by choosing to endure the same sacrifices as her people when a miners' strike in 1974 forced compulsory power cuts. Even though the palace has its own generator, the Queen insisted on working at her desk by paraffin lamp and living on a diet of hot soup and chicken salads.

When George VI became king the palace once more became a family home. The young Princesses loved exploring the endless corridors or watching the staff at work.

Queen Elizabeth, here with Air Vice Marshal 'Bomber' Harris, epitomised Britain's fighting spirit. She even used the royal garden for small arms practice.

George VI and Winston Churchill examine palace bomb damage. The attacks forged a close bond between the monarchy and the beleaguered population.

silver table decorations and seals of office, gold snuffboxes and keys as well as a menagerie of exquisitely carved Fabergé animals.

These stunning props and grandiose scenery come together for the most elaborate and memorable of royal spectaculars – the Queen's birthday parade. When the Sovereign clatters out from the courtyard of Buckingham Palace surrounded by her royal dukes and an honour guard of the Household Cavalry, this is far more than mere theatricals, what Harold Nicolson called 'the chink and glitter of scarlet and gold'.

As the monarch parades along The Mall she is symbolically defining her territorial domain and demonstrating her wider authority. Quite simply it is an exercise which illustrates the Sovereign's continuing strength within her kingdom. While Buckingham Palace is not quite a state within a state, it has many parallels with the Vatican City. Like the citadel of Catholicism, it is a closed society ruling a geographically small world but exerting an influence on national and international affairs far beyond its physical size.

Hans Christian Andersen's tale about the emperor's new clothes is often used as a metaphor to show how the monarchy has been stripped of its

The palace is a magnificent venue for entertaining. Here the Pope enjoys the Queen's hospitality.

historic authority and now parades naked, its popularity and position sustained by the self-delusion of the public. This allusion is deceptive. While the wardrobe of monarchy may be diminished, there is still enough finery to clothe it as it proceeds along the corridors of power.

Buckingham Palace is the nerve centre of monarchy, a formidable redoubt which is careful to checkmate any moves against the Queen's dignity, privileges or prerogatives. As the former prime minister Lord Callaghan acknowledges, 'The Queen is quite right to follow every move, for without her watchfulness the monarchy would not be in the strong position it is today.'

This influence ranges from the local to the global. Throughout the centuries monarchs have exercised their jurisdiction to shape the landscape of central London. Besides building the various palaces, the construction of numerous parks and gardens is due to the foresight of the Crown. It was Queen Caroline's artistic vision that inspired the work on the Serpentine and Kensington Gardens while Queen Victoria's consort Prince Albert helped design Trafalgar Square. When Prince Charles famously criticized modernist plans for the National Gallery as a 'monstrous carbuncle' he was giving voice to concern about developments in his own backyard.

At one time the royal family were major landowners and the residue of those possessions can be seen today. The Crown Estates – which George III handed to the Government in exchange for the Civil List – administer large tracts of property in the vicinity of Buckingham Palace.

Legally the Palace also controls numerous local activities ranging from public houses to the traffic. The Board of the Green Cloth, an ancient committee of the royal Household which meets in the palace billiard room, grants licences to the publicans who manage pubs 'within the verge of the Palace'. As one licensee put it, 'The monarch wished to be able to control any unseemly happenings under the palace windows.'

Traffic around the palace is also subject to regal control. Until the 1880s vehicles were barred from the royal parks and Constitution Hill. Thereafter no traffic could pass north of Buckingham Palace when Queen Victoria was in residence and even today it has limited rights. These days London Transport is excluded from using The Mall, and on Sunday this majestic thoroughfare is closed to traffic. As one palace servant said, 'It is the Queen showing just who is in control.' When discussions took place between the British Tourist Board, the Department of the Environment, the military and Buckingham Palace to alter the timing of the Changing of the Guard ceremony, it was made clear that the Queen's personal approval was needed before any action could be taken.

Inevitably a host of famous shops and services owe their origin and distinction to their proximity to the largest occuped town house in Europe. It is no coincidence that the majority of gold By Appointment signs – which signify royal favour – lie within a two-mile radius of Buckingham Palace.

Several times a week for example the royal brougham pulls up outside the bankers Coutts and Co. in the Strand. A coachman waits while a liveried messenger exchanges correspondence with the bankers who have served the royal family since George III's reign. When Princess Diana was due to dine with the Royal Hampshire Regiment of which she is colonel-in-chief she visited her husband's outfitters Gieves and Hawkes on Savile Row where she was fitted for an officer's mess jacket. If a member of the royal family wants the latest bestseller their staff are dispatched to Hatchards on Piccadilly – the only booksellers with four royal warrants.

The palace itself, with a community of 300 or so, is rather like a good-sized village with its own post offices, police station, hospital wing and, in the royal mews, a doctor's surgery. In times of crisis the Queen can quite legitimately call on her private army, the Household Division, which is based a cavalry charge away at Knightsbridge barracks. These seven regiments undertake ceremonial duties, while their young officers are used as conversational cannon fodder at social gatherings.

Occasionally the guard is called out for real. When a lone gunman attempted to kidnap Princess Anne and Captain Mark Phillips on The Mall, the army moved rapidly into action. In the confusion it was feared that an attempted coup was in progress. Palace staff watched from their windows in astonishment as armoured vehicles from the

The Queen, who keeps in close touch with European monarchs, greets Queen Beatrix of the Netherlands.

Knightsbridge barracks ringed the royal residence, armed flak-jacketed soldiers taking up strategic positions.

Indeed within the Household Division there is a hand-picked body of officers and men whose job is to protect the royal family during a crisis. This elite group, known as the Coates Mission, were set up during the Second World War when it was feared that Nazi paratroopers would land on the palace lawns and try to capture the royal family.

There is a lighter side. On one occasion the Queen accompanied her footman and corgis for a moonlight stroll round the gardens. In the time-honoured fashion a guard challenged them, shouting 'Who goes there?' The monarch said drily, 'One Queen, one footman and eight corgis,' and proceeded on her way.

The obvious physical defence of the Queen and the royal family on the outside is matched by a constant battle on the inside to ensure that the interests of the Sovereign are properly served. This is why Buckingham Palace, while the best-known building in the land, is the most secretive institution. Those who live and work there enter a self-contained society, a curious kingdom which

The splendid Gold State Coach, housed in the Royal Mews, has been used at every coronation since that of George IV.

tenaciously preserves its mystique and its traditions while steadfastly dealing with the outside world on its own terms.

The Queen's secretariat, invariably career diplomats, smoothly repulses those who seek to change the regal status quo. During this reign legislators have attempted to repeal various laws relating to the monarchy. However moves to abolish titles, the Act of Succession and the Royal Marriages Act have all failed, skilfully outmanoeuvred by an institution that invented the old boy network.

The Labour MP Tony Benn found to his cost the difficulty of attacking the royal citadel once the drawbridge has been pulled up. When he was postmaster general he wanted to delete the Queen's head from the postage stamps. He pursued his campaign tenaciously, once spending 40 minutes discussing changes with the Queen. She got down on her hands and knees in her study as he spread out revised designs. The indefatigable politician spent months lobbying, cajoling and arguing – but to no avail. George V's stricture that the Sovereign's head should always stay on a stamp was upheld and Benn, his energy and patience spent, moved to another department.

The Sovereign, who does have the advantage of seeing the prime minister in a private audience at the palace each Tuesday night, exercises her political influence in accordance with her constitutional rights which are 'to be consulted, to encourage, and to warn'. Her attention to the detail of government is legendary and her shrewd common sense has earned her the plaudits of every prime minister to have served her. 'I was struck, as everyone is, by her superior knowledge of affairs,' recalls Harold Evans, the former editor of the London *Times*. While not formally educated, her access to the levers of authority has given the Queen sharpness of observation that can startle. As one American diplomat noted with awe, 'I have learnt a lot from her. She's what we'd call "street smart".'

For a woman who has never actually walked alone down a street in her life this is quite an achievement. It underlines the breathtaking variety of confidential information which is channelled into the head office of what George V called 'the family Firm'. Locally there is a network of Lord Lieutenants, the Queen's personal representatives in each British county, who feed back opinion from the shires. Besides her weekly audience with the prime minister the Queen also has daily access to the renowned red leather boxes containing secret state papers which are sent to her from various ministries. Internationally the Foreign Office send her confidential telegrams while diplomatic bags from Commonwealth countries regularly arrive to give the Queen an insider's perspective on the nations where she is head of state.

Hand in hand with her unparalleled overview of civic and political affairs is the Queen's access to the military and ecclesiastical worlds. In the India Room at the palace is an office used by the Defence Services Secretary, a senior officer seconded from one of the three services in rotation to liaise between the monarchy and the services. The Queen's knowledge of Church matters is such that her former prime minister Lord Stockton conceded, 'She knew more about the Church than me.' This is not surprising as every newly appointed bishop visits Buckingham Palace to make his homage to the Queen.

Until 1968 the Lord Chamberlain, the head of the royal Household, was the official censor of all plays which were to be performed publicly in Britain. It was his job to ensure that nothing 'unsuitable or blasphemous' was licensed. While this function has ceased, the gimlet eye of the Palace still surveys the social and commercial scene to ensure that the Queen's name is never taken in vain. For the weddings of the Prince and Princess of Wales and the Duke and Duchess of York, the Lord Chamberlain's Office vetted official wedding mugs, tea towels, postcards and other paraphernalia to ensure it met suitably dignified standards.

Manufacturers who try to sell their goods on the back of the royal family's name quickly receive a terse warning letter from the Palace while those such as dress designers who supply goods and services to the royal family are under strict instructions to remain discreet.

The State Opening of Parliament is the only occasion when the Queen reads a speech written by someone else, namely the prime minister. However the Sovereign exerts her influence in other ways.

Health guru Joe Corvo, who uses the ancient Chinese technique of zone therapy on the Duchess of York and the Princess of Wales, was ticked off by the Palace for 'royal namedropping' when discussing his work. From television commercials to teeshirts, books to ballgowns, the palace courtiers are ever vigilant.

The royal family themselves are enthusiastic participants in this process – especially with regard to personal publicity in the mass media. Princess Margaret was so incensed when she read a newspaper story about her friendship with a young man that she sent an angry memo to the palace press office. She wrote: 'Here is the article. I haven't read it all for it's too nauseating.'

Indeed, like any large corporation, the Palace attempts a comprehensive control to ensure the continuing privacy and propriety of the royal family. The regulated release of information is an in-

tegral part of this process – as the Duchess of York learned to her cost.

When she and Prince Andrew posed for a series of family photographs taken by Prince Andrew's friend, American cameraman Gene Nocon, for the Spanish-owned magazine *Hello!*, the palace authorities were not amused. It was not the sight of the Duchess changing baby Princess Eugenie's nappy or feeding Princess Beatrice that alarmed them but the fact that they had been kept in the dark about the deal.

The Duchess was summoned to see the Queen's private secretary Sir Robert Fellowes for a brisk dressing down. However, as the Duchess complained to her friends afterwards, the photo session, which was roundly criticized as 'tacky', was the Duke's idea – but he had returned to his Royal Navy ship before the storm broke.

Urbane discretion and cultivated caution are the hallmarks of those who serve the Queen in a senior capacity. Secrecy comes with the seals of office. Just to make sure, all staff are legally bound to remain silent about their work in royal service. Even the legendary MI5 spymaster Peter Wright failed to penetrate that armour when he closely questioned Anthony Blunt, a former Communist spy and Surveyor of the Queen's Pictures.

During his inquiry, Wright was called to the palace to see the Queen's then private secretary Sir Michael Adeane. Adeane told him, 'From time to time you may find Blunt referring to an assignment he undertook on behalf of the Palace – a visit to Germany at the end of the war. Please do not pursue the matter. Strictly speaking it is not relevant to the considerations of national security.'

Wright admitted that even though he spent hundreds of hours with Blunt, the royal courtier never gave a hint about his secret mission. He recorded, with rueful admiration, 'The Palace have had several centuries to learn the difficult art of scandal burying. MI5 have only been in the business since 1909.' In fact Blunt's task was to recover documents, known as the Marburg File, which related to the Duke of Windsor's relations with the Nazis.

The behind-the-scenes work of the Palace exists not only to protect the interests of the British royal family but to advance the cause of monarchy throughout Europe. Indeed Buckingham Palace, which could properly be described as the headquarters of international monarchy, is enjoying an unparalleled period of influence and prestige.

For the House of Windsor is the secret leader of an emerging freemasonry of European royalty. Every two years the private secretaries of the crowned heads of the major European monarchies meet in a private, closed session. They discuss the issues concerning modern monarchy and decide a common policy. When the fourth such meeting was held in Madrid, at the instigation of the Dutch royal family, discussions ranged from how to cope with excessive press intrusion – a particular concern of the Queen – to the proposed sale by Christie's the auctioneers of a Norwegian royal family order, the Grand Croisette of St Olaf.

As Herr Flaxstadt, the Norwegian court marshal, observed, 'It is an old boys' club. We discuss official visits, protocol questions and the numerous bureaucratic matters which arise during the course of our work. Although we cannot make decisions we do make recommendations to our respective Heads of State.'

Indeed the existence of this shadowy royal club highlights the informal and semi-formal network of contacts between the various European royal Houses – and illustrates the considerable influence exerted by royalty in a changing Europe. Like all the best clubs, the league of royalty has its own codes and language. If for example the Queen sends a letter to King Juan Carlos of Spain it will be written in cryptic language known only to the monarchs themselves. It is a throwback to the days when all royal communication was by sealed letter and delivered by trusted horsemen.

The Queen and the Prince of Wales in concert with King Juan Carlos of Spain have been active in co-ordinating moves to restore monarchies in newly democratic eastern bloc countries. In particular they arranged a visit to Geneva, Switzerland so that Crown Prince Alexander of Yugoslavia could meet government officials from his home country.

He said, 'I have maintained close contact with the British royal family and other royal families.

In her early days at the palace Princess Diana surprised many staff by visiting the kitchens for a chat.

During their reign, George VI and the Queen Mother dined in the Chinese Dining Room.

An exchange of information and dialogue has taken place in a very calm and mature way as it would between members of any family. Her Majesty and Prince Charles have been particularly helpful.'

This heady activity is a world removed from the traditional work of the palace staff – organizing garden parties, receptions and investitures as well as planning royal visits and formal occasions such as the State Opening of Parliament. 'I am commanded by the Queen's corgis to thank the children for their very thoughtful and delicious present of biscuits which were greatly appreciated,' wrote the Sovereign's deputy private secretary after one successful visit, showing that straight-faced humour and prompt courtesy are qualities as necessary to the successful courtier as diplomatic finesse.

During the day the palace is a hum of quietly civilized activity as the staff ensure that the machinery of monarchy continues its smooth pro-

gress. Writer Douglas Keay vividly remembers his own visit to see Prince Philip. He recalls, 'As you follow the footman, whose pace gives no chance to linger, you may quite possibly overhear brief snatches of quite intriguing telephone conversations. Phrases such as "I was speaking to the Queen about that this morning" or "I don't think the Duke of Edinburgh has anything booked for that particular evening but I'll check." '

However beneath the surface of mandarin calm, the jostling for place and advantage is the same as in any other civil service department. The only consolation is that when the knives are out they are solid silver and date back to George III. It is a place of rumour, gossip and hearsay where, as one member of staff says, 'You can have a cold in the morning and be dead of AIDS by mid-afternoon.' Traditionally office doors are left open, probably to catch the drift of rumour floating along the corridors. In such a closed community, where everyone lives in each other's pockets, there are few secrets.

During the hunt by Scotland Yard detectives to find the thief who stole letters sent to Princess Anne by the Queen's equerry Commander Timothy Laurence, even the Queen's then private secretary Sir William Heseltine was taken aback by the number of palace staff who were fully aware of this 'confidential' relationship. He would be just as surprised by the number of staff who discuss the possible identity of a secret admirer who, just before Christmas, sends Princess Anne a red rose which is taken to her rooms with her morning cup of Queen Mary tea.

Indeed outsiders, such as hapless Commonwealth diplomats seconded to the palace for a short period, are baffled by the byzantine hierarchy of rules and relationships. At first sight it is the 'Upstairs' staff of members of the Household and the officials – the royal equivalent of board directors and line managers – who run the show while the 'Downstairs' staff are there to obey instructions. In the looking-glass world of royalty things are never quite as they seem.

Dressers and valets for example, who attend to the daily requirements of their royal principals, have more influence than their humble titles suggest. These royal Jeeveses are the only staff to

Guest bedroom number 236 in the Belgian Suite is allocated to visiting VIPs and royalty.

have immediate access to the royal family (even the Queen's private secretary must have an appointment) and they act as a daily bellweather to test the royal temperament. An officious member of the Household can find his life made difficult by a trusted servant.

The unspoken reign of these senior servants is matched only by the empires they command. For instance a housekeeper can pick up a towel in Prince Edward's bedroom but not his slippers – that is a job for the valet. However the valet is not allowed to turn back the bed or pull the curtains – that is the housekeeper's domain.

While working practices have moved on since the days of Queen Victoria when one servant was responsible for laying the fire and another for lighting it, demarcation lines are time honoured and rigidly enforced. When Princess Diana tried to loosen these boundaries she found that she was frustrated at every turn. 'We don't run our staff, they run us,' she said in exasperation.

In the early days of her royal career, Diana discovered to her cost that Buckingham Palace is a world of lilliputian kingdoms where even a fairy-tale princess is unwelcome. Before her wedding she

regularly visited the kitchens to while away a few minutes in idle conversation. Barefoot, wearing jeans and a sweater, she helped with the washing up and, on one famous occasion, buttered the toast for a junior footman. However her excursions behind the green baize door irritated several chefs who felt she was spying and concerned the Queen who realized, quite rightly, that the royal innocent at large had not learned the niceties of palace life.

Tactfully the Queen asked her to resist these visits as it was upsetting the subtle equilibrium that exists between Upstairs and Downstairs. These days Diana occasionally visits the staff in the kitchen and, even after ten years, still alarms them with the informal way she casually sits on the wooden pastry table, eager to catch up with the latest gossip.

Indeed it is this framework of unspoken rules, the values which define monarchy, which have elevated Buckingham Palace to the status of an international institution. Architecturally the Queen's home has a cumbersome majesty – 'a ponderous Palace' as royal photographer Cecil Beaton said – while the interiors have a certain

The 150-foot-long Picture Gallery was remodelled by Queen Mary whose energy revitalized the palace.

sonorous splendour, careworn with the practised polish of a thousand performances.

However the palace has a symbolic quality that transcends its physical frontiers. Just as the Queen's life is remote from everyday experience, so the palace is a world removed from the routine. The master of the Household Sir Paul Greening often smiles to himself when he telephones unsuspecting guests to invite them to lunch with the Sovereign. Many think the request is a hoax and need days to be convinced.

Headmistress Joy Pinder, who attended a recent palace lunch, recalls, 'The call came out of the blue. I thought it was my husband's police colleagues pulling my leg. A very well-spoken gentleman told me that the Queen had heard about my work and would I like to have lunch with her. I said, "Don't be bloody stupid" and told him to write. It was only when I received the official letter that it sunk in. I mean these things just don't happen to people like us.'

The continuing skill of the modern monarchy has been the successful sleight of hand which manages to transform this remote reality into a vision of gracious approachability.

It is this delicate balance of common humanity and an unattainable mystique that contributes to the magnetism of the monarchy. In this spirit Buckingham Palace is universally regarded as the court of last resort, the fount of natural justice. A proportion of the 75,000 letters which the Palace receives each year are appeals for help. The complaints of prison inmates, the protests of council tenants and begging letters from pensioners asking for money are typical. A group of residents in a Rugby old people's home for example appealed to the Queen to protect their 'peace and security' when the local council wanted to shut their Mill Green nursing home to save money.

Most letters are sent to the relevant government department although occasionally the Queen exercises her influence. Her letter replying to the grieving mother of a victim of the notorious Yorkshire Ripper was effective in stopping the dubious practice of newspapers making payments to the murderer's relatives. On another occasion the Queen Mother played Cupid between a lovesick Scottish girl who had written to the palace and her boy-friend, a Polish soldier. The Queen Mother sent her letter to the Polish embassy which contacted the squaddie. Happily the couple eventually married.

This image of approachability reached an extreme in the summer of 1982 when an unemployed north London labourer Michael Fagan broke into the palace so that he could speak to the Queen about his personal troubles.

He now recalls, 'When I got to Buckingham Palace I wanted the Queen to be my ideal woman, this woman who lived in splendid isolation. I wanted her to be the woman I could communicate with, who would understand me and my everyday aspirations. I wanted her to know me. I could have gone to the Sultan of Brunei for instance but it's not the same as the Queen of England. This woman is the pinnacle of our society, the summit of our dreams. We are tribal animals and the Queen is the head of the tribe. I wanted to speak to our chieftain.'

Indeed the Queen recognizes her mythical status. She has remarked to friends that she is seen as a 'Jungian archetype', a concept developed by the psychologist Carl Jung which means in this case that society projects its dreams of motherhood, justice and leadership on to the figure of the monarch. Others have tried to capture this universal attraction. When the artist Pietro Annigoni was working on his famous portrait of the Queen he explained his vision of her. At the end of one sitting he told her, 'I see Your Majesty as being condemned to solitude because of your position. As a wife and mother you are entirely different but I see you really alone as a monarch . . . if I succeed, the woman, the Queen and, for that matter, the solitude will emerge.'

This profound spiritual appeal is most forcefully expressed at times of national tribulation and celebration. Buckingham Palace – rather than the Palace of Westminster – is the natural focal point for outpourings of joy or sorrow. The day after the attempted kidnap of Princess Anne in The Mall, a *Times* leader went so far as to describe the palace as the centre of the nation's 'inner spiritual life' – a far cry from the day in the early part of this century when parliament considered selling the building for housing.

The monarchy is the fount of all honour and the palace the natural setting for investitures to confer awards on outstanding citizens. Prince Charles has conducted several ceremonies in place of the Queen.

This sentiment is best expressed at a royal wedding. As a wedding is a universal symbol of union, it is perhaps inevitable that a royal marriage has gained international appeal. Television has made us all global villagers and so when the local squire gets married, interest is worldwide. It was no surprise that millions more viewers watched the union of the Prince of Wales and Lady Diana Spencer than tuned in to the first moon landing.

Buckingham Palace was the natural setting, the mood of exuberance spilling from The Mall into the royal family's home. Prince Charles vividly remembers the scene. 'It really was remarkable and I found myself standing at the window with tears pouring down my face. Inevitably these things don't always last very long but I think it made one realize that underneath everything else, all the rowing and the bickering and disagreements that go on the rest of the time, every now and then you get a reason for a celebration or a feeling of being a nation.'

If constitutional monarchy is the symbolic focus for certain ideals of family and national life, then Buckingham Palace is the material setting for this tribal dream. The staff who work there are not just directors, producers and scene shifters for what Professor Edmund Leach calls 'the irrational theatre of monarchy'; they are also the keepers of that dream. Labour politician Richard Crossman sensed the deeper purpose of the palace after he had taken his children round the state rooms. He wrote, 'Interesting the effect on them. They are usually bouncing and ebullient. Strangely enough I

The wedding of the Prince and Princess of Wales symbolizes the global appeal of the royal family and underlines the palace's position as the perfect setting for ceremonial events.

think the children were really impressed. It looked and felt like the kind of palace they had dreamed of and they were a bit solemn inside.'

Indeed Buckingham Palace is home to our collective vision of the monarchy, an institution

By royal standards, the wedding of the Duke and Duchess of York was an informal affair. Photographer Albert Watson caught the mood, using a brass horn to bring the royal family to order.

which is at once familiar and mysterious, a place of intriguing illusion and everyday domesticity where regal grandeur is accompanied by a handbag, a scamper of corgis and a smile. It is the ultimate home for the ultimate family.

II

AT HOME WITH THE ROYAL FAMILY

*I*t was the heart-stopping moment every parent dreads. As Princess Diana casually towelled her blonde hair after her morning swim, she noticed that the swimming pool was ominously quiet.

While her girlfriend made idle chitchat, Diana saw a motionless figure lying face down in the bottom of the pool. It was her elder son, Prince William. Without pausing to strip off her white towelling dressing gown and track suit, she ran to the edge of the pool and dived in, swimming frantically towards the lifeless figure.

Her lungs bursting and heart racing, she grabbed the future king and dragged him to the surface. As William reached the side he was convulsed – with laughter. The mischievous Prince, who learned to swim as a toddler, had played dead in order to give his mother a fright. He succeeded. Diana said afterwards, 'It scared me to death seeing William like that. I was in such a panic I thought my heart was going to explode it was pounding so hard.'

In those few moments of alarm, the Princess, who ironically uses the pool at Buckingham Palace to relax, realized in full the onerous responsibility of bringing up a son who is to be the future king of Britain and heir to the Windsor dynasty.

The palace nursery was once home for Prince Edward and Prince Andrew. Today it is occupied by Princesses Beatrice and Eugenie.

Indeed the art of bringing up children as members of the royal family is difficult enough without these deliberate alarms. It is a life in which royal children soon discover that time with their parents is rationed, servants act as surrogate mothers or fathers and the values of caution, consideration and duty take precedence over personal pleasures and desires. Royal children very quickly learn to mask their true feelings, to construct a personal armour that parries the intrusive question and deflects the public insult.

While friends may empathize, only the royal family truly understands the peculiar pleasures of growing up in a palace. Royal secrets and problems are shared within the immediate family. Ultimately trust lies in the blood. As Prince Charles says, 'I think of my family as very special people. I have never wanted not to have a home life – to get away from home . . . I am happier at home, with my family, than anywhere else.'

As home to the royal family, Buckingham Palace is a safe haven where children can play peacefully, where bachelor princes can conduct their romantic assignations in secret and where the Sovereign can set aside the burdens of her office and relax.

For Prince Charles the palace is filled with happy memories. Like most of the royal family, he was born there. He chose a candlelit dinner in his second-floor rooms as a suitable venue to ask Lady Diana Spencer to be his bride. They celebrated their wedding with a splendid lunchtime breakfast – as it is called – for their royal relations, while their first child Prince William was christened in the Music Room like previous generations.

For nearly a decade the second-floor nursery had been used intermittently as a breakfast room by Princess Anne, Prince Edward and the Duke and Duchess of York. Now these five rooms ring to the sound of childish laughter and babble as the Duchess of York's daughters, Princess Beatrice, now three, and eighteen-month-old Princess Eugenie enjoy their upbringing within the palace.

The Duchess has largely forsaken her isolated country home on the edge of Windsor Great Park which the Queen had built as a wedding present. She has told friends that, with Prince Andrew often away at sea on naval duties, she feels 'nervous' about living on her own yet finds the spy cameras and other security devices 'intrusive'.

For the Duchess, who now lives in Prince Charles's old apartment, the palace is comforting and socially convenient – but none too comfortable. It may have been suitable for a royal bachelor but is rather too cosy for a growing family. The outsize mahogany wardrobes and chests-of-drawers which were once adequate for a Navy lifestyle are ill-suited to a bustling young woman who is constantly on parade. The corridor outside their apartment is littered with dress rails, suitcases, and hatboxes as her dresser Jane Andrews and housekeeper Mandy Young attempt to make sense out of the chaos of clothing.

Such is the extra workload placed on the palace staff that the number of nursery footmen has been doubled to cater for the needs of the Duchess and her family. She is fortunate that the nursery is next door to her office so that she can mix work with children's games. Occasionally they are complementary. The Duchess closely followed the story of two-year-old Tamara Rainey who underwent two life-saving liver transplants at Addenbrooke's Hospital, Cambridge. She encouraged Beatrice to sit at the large wooden table in the nursery and paint the little girl her own get well card. It had the desired effect. 'It was a real tonic and such a surprise,' said her mother, Marina.

However when the Duchess is working – she starts her day with a vigorous workout at six in the

Prince Charles with his model horse and trap which is now used by a new generation of royal children.

morning – the girls are looked after by nannies Alison Wardley and Caroline Grinnell. The days may be gone when a nanny dressed her royal charges in their best clothes before they were presented to their parents, but there is a formality about the nursery routine. It is something Prince Andrew insists upon.

The Princesses' nannies are always in uniform as is the liveried footman who lays the girls' breakfast table with miniature silver cutlery before picking up their shoes and boots for cleaning. Breakfast follows at 8.00 a.m., lunch at 12.30 and the girls are bathed and dressed for bed before the Duchess comes in to see them at 7.30 p.m. The girls' weekly menu, which is drawn up by the palace chef and approved by nanny, is prepared in the kitchen nearly a quarter of a mile away and brought up in a heated trolley. There is a kitchen near by for making snacks and hot drinks.

When Prince Andrew's valet Michael Perry calls in to the nursery he finds that little has changed since the days when he was the nursery footman. Michael, who has a reputation for organizing exotic card games in his palace quarters, was largely responsible for the upbringing of Princes Andrew and Edward. 'He taught them the facts of life, how to behave and how to look after themselves,' recalls a former colleague. 'He never deferred to them and they respected him for that.'

In his day the Princes played soccer or rode their tricycles along the nursery corridor. 'Every now and again a pane of glass got broken but I don't think we ever broke a piece of Meissen or anything like that,' recalls Prince Andrew.

The Coronation coach in its glass case that stands in the hallway, the tired wooden rocking horse by the nursery lift, and the rather battered upright piano and settee have lasted from Prince Charles's childhood. These days it is the the building bricks, the pink rocking elephant and Beatrix Potter books that attract childish interest.

The Duchess is fortunate that so many of her friends like Clare Wentworth-Stanley and Julia Dodd-Noble have children the same age as her own. It means that the Princesses do not suffer the same fate as so many royal children – a surfeit of adult company. Birthday celebrations are a frequent event as a stream of the Duchess's chums bring their offspring for a party at the palace.

The usual fare is jam pennies, honey sandwiches and chicken sandwiches washed down with soft drinks. Chef prepares a birthday cake – a favourite is a chocolate hedgehog – for the festivities.

This relaxed regime – the Duchess likes her staff to be casually dressed outside the palace grounds – is a far cry from the days when Princess Anne was scolded when she refused to curtsy to 'gan gan', her childhood name for Queen Mary.

Indeed the Queen may rather envy her daughter-in-law's relative freedom. She was away on a visit to Australia and New Zealand for so long that Prince Charles had learned to read by the time she arrived home. Early in her reign the demands of the position meant that she saw so little of her eldest son and daughter that she asked the then prime minister Winston Churchill to put back by an hour the weekly Tuesday night audience so that she could spend time in the nursery.

With her 'second family' of Andrew and Edward the Queen was more relaxed. On Wednesday nights she babysat so that nanny Mabel Anderson could enjoy an evening off duty. However there was rarely any question of the boys running down the stairs to the Queen's study. First Mabel had to ring the Queen's page to make sure the Queen was not too busy and then, after a wash and brush-up, take the boys to see their mother.

The Queen and the Duke of Edinburgh always made time to see the Princes. Even before a formal occasion such as a state banquet, the Queen, in her evening gown and tiara, would sit on the piano stool and read to Edward while Prince Philip would chat to Andrew about the day's events. 'They were just like an ordinary family,' recalls one former palace servant, with unintentional irony.

Certainly the Duke is very much the head of the family – even though, as consort, he must always walk in the Queen's shadow. 'He was didactic in a gentle way and never as aggressive in private as his abrasive public image,' say staff. While nursery staff were not allowed to chastise their charges, their parents certainly did.

On one occasion the Queen and the Duke arrived as nanny Anderson and the boys were watching the long-running television soap opera 'Coronation Street', about life in a working-class street in the north of England. Blowzy barmaid Bet Lynch was in the midst of a rowdy argument with a customer at the Rover's Return pub when Prince Andrew commented disdainfully, 'Oh God, look at all those common people.' His father reprimanded him immediately. He clipped the royal teenager round the ear and told him sternly, 'If it wasn't for people like that you would not be sitting here.' For once the talkative Prince was silent.

The Queen's onerous duties meant that she saw little of Prince Charles and Princess Anne during their early years.

Usually it was Edward who was the quiet prince, content to sit happily at his desk, reading books on composers or classics like Kipling, Dickens and Shakespeare. A favourite game was to listen to the classical music station, BBC Radio 3, and identify the various composers before they were announced. He was rather jealous when the Queen of Denmark gave his brother a Bang and Olufsen stereo system and a collection of classical records. To rub salt into the wound, Andrew never used it.

His decision to join the Royal Marines surprised everyone who knew him. Edward, who disliked rough games, had talked of going into the City. Indeed his only interest in the military was helping his brother make model planes.

By contrast Andrew, boisterous, arrogant and energetic, raced noisily around the nursery floor, chatting to housemaids or favoured visitors like the Queen's lady-in-waiting Susan Hussey who regularly popped along from her nearby office. At rare moments of calm he amused himself by flicking through books on royal regiments or comics like *The Beano* and *Dandy*. The Princes were not totally alone. For a time they were joined in the nursery quarters by Princess Tanya of Hanover, the granddaughter of Prince Philip's sister, who lived at the palace whilst studying in London.

While the boys had few friends their own age – apart from the Mountbatten clan – and little in common, they loved their days in the nursery. The return to Gordonstoun School in the far north of Scotland always filled Prince Edward with foreboding.

Everyone knew when term was about to begin as Edward would conveniently develop a sudden cold and try to stay on at the palace. One occasion was particularly poignant. The young Prince, smartly attired in his school uniform, simply refused to go. He clung to his brass bedstead before being prised away by the nursery footman. Then he held fast to the rail of the nursery lift. Neither nanny Anderson, the footman nor the royal chauffeur could console the sobbing Prince. The Queen was called and, after a few motherly words, he agreed to leave. When she had kissed and waved him goodbye, the Sovereign turned to her staff and said, 'That was very painful indeed.'

However that long-term decision to send her children to school, albeit public boarding establishments, is seen by historians as one of the central achievements of the Queen's reign. Her biographer Lady Longford argues, 'The fact that their children have mixed with ordinary children all their lives has made other reforms much easier for them than they were for their parents.'

This relatively liberal upbringing enjoyed by the Queen's children is matched by the relaxed exercise of her authority during their adult lives. As a long-standing friend of the Queen explains, 'The Queen does not see herself as a matriarchal figure. They all live their lives in separate compartments.'

While they are a close family, they are not a dropping-in family. Unlike the days of Queen Victoria or George V, the royal family does not dine together. On those infrequent occasions when the family is off duty and in residence at the palace they will usually dine separately.

They have their own establishments and circles of friends, so conversations are limited to brief

A cloud of paperwork, pens and photographs covers Princess Elizabeth's desk while a corgi lazes at her feet. Pink carnations are still her favourite blooms.

talks on the intercom system. Daily domestic intercourse which involves a shouted request in ordinary houses is by handwritten memo.

For example they all subscribe to homeopathic medicine and take black leather cases of powders and potions with them on their travels. These natural cures range from white arsenic, snake's venom and deadly nightshade to arnica cream for bumps and bruises sustained whilst out riding. There is much swapping and changing, as this memo from Prince Charles to his staff shows:

> Please resupply me with the following. A tube of Redoxon tablets. Tube of Arnica ointment since the Queen has borrowed my tube. Much needed before skiing.

This royal version of the grapevine works in other ways. When Australian physiotherapist Sarah Key arrived in London from her home in Sydney she soon built up a royal clientele. Personal recommendation meant that she started treating Princess Margaret's former husband Lord Snowdon, then Prince Charles and finally Princess Diana, who has long suffered from a bad back.

A few words from the wise have helped Prince Edward conduct his romantic life with an anonymity that his older brothers could only dream about. In his bachelor days Prince Charles used false names, addresses and different titles to throw photographers off the scent, once travelling under the name of Charlie Chester. As the Earl of Chester he was quite entitled to use this surname.

He passed on advice to his brothers, as Prince Andrew once admitted to a group of journalists. 'Charles has told me what to expect from you lot. I shall be on my guard,' he said. While Buckingham Palace is viewed as a safe haven, caution is still the watchword when love is in the air. During his romance with the American actress Koo Stark, Prince Andrew frequently travelled from Buckingham Palace in disguise. On one occasion he fooled the neighbours at Koo's Kensington home by dressing as a traffic warden; on another he arrived in the guise of a milkman.

When Koo called him at the palace she used the code name Fiona Campbell. If she wrote she put initials on the bottom left-hand corner of the letter so that it would only be opened by him. It is a

A family discussion over lunch. Even when dining privately certain formalities are observed. The Queen's children always bow or curtsy to her.

royal custom. During the Prince's romance with Sandi Jones, a Canadian girl he met during his schooldays, he wrote the initial 'A' on the envelope so that her family and flatmates would know to leave it alone.

On Sarah Ferguson's visits to Andrew's palace apartment she and her flatmate Carolyn Cotterell, now her principal lady-in-waiting, had a well-rehearsed routine. Carolyn checked the roads around the palace to ensure there were no lurking photographers and then she would use her car headlights to flash the all clear to Sarah who quickly drove into the gravel forecourt.

Unlike his brothers, Prince Edward has cultivated an anonymous public persona which enables him to walk from his palace apartment to his theatrical offices in Soho without being recognized. He likes to tell the story of the teenage girl who did a double take when she spotted him walking along The Mall. 'Ooh look, there's Prince Andrew,' she called out to her friends.

He has conducted his romantic life with a similar discretion, aware that an innocent cup of tea and plate of sandwiches with a female colleague in his palace rooms could well turn into banner headlines the following day. When he invites a girlfriend to the palace he will only inform his valet. His job is to organize the meal and alert the police on the gate about the Prince's visitor. Occasionally even these services are dispensed with. Palace staff still recall the day Koo Stark appeared unannounced in the kitchens to prepare a picnic lunch for herself and Prince Andrew.

When Edward is entertaining his girlfriends, be it model Romy Adlington, millionaire's daughter Georgia May or television journalist Anastasia Cooke, a familiar pattern emerges. Once inside the palace the young lady is met at the Prince of Wales Door by the Prince's valet, taken in the lift to the royal drawing room and then made comfortable. When the Prince is entertaining informally his valet puts up a card table covered with a linen cloth and leaves a cold collation, usually chicken and roast beef, on the side. Before the royal Jeeves discreetly retires he ensures that the fridge in the

The Duke and Duchess of York now occupy Prince Charles's apartments. The Duchess prefers the comforts of Buckingham Palace to her new home.

Prince's room has a supply of German wine and Malvern water.

Sometimes the path to true love does not run so smoothly. One Thursday evening Prince Charles invited the actress Susan George to join him for supper at the palace. As it was the night before a planned shooting weekend on the Queen's Sandringham estate, his labrador gun dog Sandringham Harvey was allowed in the apartment. Shortly before Susan George arrived, Charles's valet went into his routine. He took a nursery trolley to the kitchens and collected a cold supper of chicken in aspic and an assortment of salads. While the Prince dressed, his valet laid the table, leaving the trolley in the drawing room.

On his return he discovered Harvey polishing off the Prince's romantic dinner for two. Fortunately the Prince saw the funny side and the royal chef was able to rustle up a second meal in the frantic minutes before Charles's date arrived.

Lady Diana Spencer enjoyed her first supper with the Prince following a performance of Verdi's *Requiem* – one of her favourite works – at the Royal Albert Hall. With her grandmother, Ruth, Lady Fermoy as their chaperone, that recital on 17 July 1979 marked the beginning of the royal romance of the decade.

His memo to his then valet, the late Stephen Barry, relating to the meeting is typical of the elaborate planning for a royal date. It reads:

> Please ring Captain Anthony Asquith before going out shooting and tell him that I have asked Lady Diana Spencer (Lady Fermoy's granddaughter) to come to the Albert Hall and dinner afterwards at BP on Sunday evening. Please ask him if this can be arranged and she will arrive with her grandmother at the Albert Hall. If it is allright please ask him to ring back at lunchtime when we will be in the House. C.

While royal romance adds spice to palace life, usually the royal apartments are the venue for entertaining friends or officials from the various charities associated with a royal personage. Prince Edward, whose civil list allowance was increased to £100,000 ($180,000) a year to allow for his new duties as head of the Duke of Edinburgh award scheme, regularly entertains the organization's leading lights or potential donors. Such is his workload – dividing his time between his theatrical career and the award scheme – that his staff fear for his health.

Prince Charles, who now lives at Kensington Palace, still uses the House when he wants to impress the wealthy businessmen he likes to lassoo into his various schemes. After one dinner to raise funds for young Asians, a north London property developer who wrote out a cheque for £100,000 ($180,000) beforehand said, 'That was the most expensive meal of my life. But it was worth it.'

At these dinners the Prince, his sights firmly fixed on the horizon of substantial charity donations, is prepared to turn a blind eye to occasional breaches in etiquette. However there are limits, as an American senator discovered when he was invited to one fund-raising dinner in aid of the United World Colleges. At first he followed the protocol and called the Prince 'Your Royal Highness'. Afterwards 'Sir' is the accepted form of address. The senator felt so comfortable that he referred to the Prince as 'Charles' throughout the first two courses. The Prince became so angry that his ears started to flap – a signal for his private secretary to intervene and politely inform the politician about proper procedure.

Princess Anne faced a distinctly more unpleasant challenge to her dignity when she privately entertained 118 St John Ambulance cadets in the Music Room. As she chatted to groups of youngsters she met one teenage girl whose father had told her to 'spit in the Princess's eye because I can't stand the royal family'. The youngster said afterwards that she was so impressed by the Princess that she was going to try and change her father's views.

Normally the Princess spends as much time as possible at her Gloucestershire country home of Gatcombe Park, only staying in London if there is an evening engagement to attend. An early riser, she is normally dressed and ready for her day's events by seven o'clock, travelling in the mirrored lift to the ground floor where her ancient Reliant Scimitar – and inevitable detective – are waiting.

The Duchess of York went on a rigorous exercise regime following the birth of Princess Eugenie. She swam a mile in the palace pool every day.

Bachelor Prince Edward entertains girlfriends far more discreetly than either of his brothers.

Her reluctance to tarry long in her second-floor apartment may have something to do with her neighbours – the Duke and Duchess of York. Everyone knows when the Duchess is entertaining her chums. Her dinner parties have a reputation for lasting the longest and being the noisiest. Billy Connolly, Pamela Stephenson, David Frost, actress Priscilla Phillips and American socialite Steve Wyatt have all enjoyed her hospitality.

While her appetite for life has earned her public criticism, that generous nature means that her circle of friends is regularly treated to the pleasures of the palace. She goes to some lengths to make these occasions memorable. At her housewarming party she tricked out the dining room with fake cobwebs and plastic spiders to create a suitable Hallowe'en mood, while for Princess Beatrice's first birthday she created a miniature fairground in the gardens of Castlewood House.

Another raucous gathering, held for the benefit of the backroom workers at her wedding, ended up with late-night high jinks in the swimming pool as the Duke and Duchess encouraged their guests to jump in, clothed or not. Their evident enthusiasm came as a surprise to guests unused to seeing the royal family gleefully throwing bread rolls,

plastic fruit and bowls of sugar at each other.

After an evening out on the town – favourites are Harry's Bar in Mayfair or Annabel's nightclub – she will regularly arrive back at the palace and expect staff, who started work at six thirty in the morning, to feed everyone. Hardly surprising then that her fan club counts few members from the ranks of the Downstairs staff.

While she plays hard, the Duchess works hard with a routine that leaves her staff struggling to keep up. 'She's a great rusher,' says hairdresser Denise MacAdam, who was responsible for styling her Titian tresses on her wedding day. 'She's usually got about fifteen minutes, an hour if you're lucky.' Other friends testify, 'She flies around at a rate of knots, can't keep still for a minute.'

A frequent complaint is that she tries to cram so much into her daily diary that she has to cancel lunch with friends at short notice. She acknowledges that the downside of becoming a member of the royal family is that friends fall by the wayside and there isn't time to bring in many new faces. Priscilla Phillips, who joined her on holiday in Morocco, met her simply by introducing herself when she spotted her in a London restaurant sitting with mutual friends.

That daily royal life begins with a strenuous early morning workout based on the exercise regime devised by Callan Pinckney. The American fitness guru even flew from her New York home to supervise her royal client, spending up to three hours a day in her apartment. 'She was very dedicated to losing weight' and worked as hard as anybody I have known,' says Callan.

Those exercises together with an idiosyncratic diet have earned official plaudits from slimmers' organizations who are impressed by the way the Duchess regained her figure following the birth of Princess Eugenie. The unusual secret of her success has intrigued dieticians.

For weeks the determined Duchess lived on a diet of ten exotic fruits, like guava, mango and pineapple, together with liberal doses of sliced root ginger soaked in boiling water which she drank from a large breakfast cup. This was supplemented by a course of homeopathic vitamin pills.

The Duchess has made something of a study of diets – during her bachelor days she tried every fad on the market in an effort to control her weight – but now has allowed herself to be advised by a troika of health advisors who are responsible for her much admired figure. For several years she has visited the Harley Street clinic of Gudrun Johnsson, a Swedish expert in reflexology and homeopathy, and zone therapist Joe Corvo – known as Joe the Toe because he massages the feet, as well as Callan Pinckney.

An escape from the royal routine favoured by the Duchess and Princess Diana is a long swim in the palace pool. After the birth of Princess Eugenie, the Duchess regularly swam a mile a day to help tone her figure. These sessions are a brief respite from the tyranny of the timetable.

As a senior director in the family firm, the Duchess finds that the nuts and bolts of royal life involve an endless succession of meetings and memos. 'Notes, notes, always notes,' says the Duchess as she tries to juggle requests for official engagements, charity meetings and overseas visits.

Unlike company directors in other walks of life, the obscure demands of royal life mean dressing in full evening attire at ten o'clock in the morning for a sculptor or portrait painter. The remorseless royal schedule doesn't make life any easier for the artist either.

When artist Michael Noakes decided to paint the Duke and Duchess together – and holding hands as well – he doubled the timetable difficulties. He solved the problem by tracing the feet of the royal couple on to a rectangular piece of hardboard so at least they could adopt the correct pose for the following sitting.

The Queen, as chairman of the board, has even less time than her directors – or her artists. When Noakes was commissioned to paint her one of the first things she said to him when she arrived in the Yellow Drawing Room was that she 'really must do something about the curtains'. Fabric swatches were duly ordered and the next time he came various samples were lying on the sofas. 'But four years later, when I next went back to paint her, the samples were still there. She hadn't had time to do anything about it,' he said.

Such is the pressure on her time that she has her own gift room, next to her dining room, where she chooses presents for weddings, christenings and

Christmas so that she does not have to waste effort shopping. Indeed Christmas is a particularly painful time for the Sovereign. There are so many functions and so many hands to shake that she is often seen wringing her hands, rather like Lady Macbeth, as she tries to ease the soreness in finger joints afflicted by rheumatoid arthritis.

Yet in spite of these endless pressures, palace staff testify that, of all the members of the royal family, she is the least exacting and therefore the easiest to care for. Certainly she is the most respected. As one long-serving member of staff admits, 'Each time I see her to receive my Christmas present my knees turn to jelly even though I've done it so many times in the past.'

It is this constant juxtaposition of simple domestic routine in a gilded setting that is a source of such curiosity. Children who write to the Queen invariably want to know about her crown and her furnishings. 'Are the toilet seats in Buckingham Palace made of gold?' asked eleven-year-old Vanessa Freeman.

In fact the Queen's apartments eschew grandeur in favour of comfort and utility. She may well be described as the world's richest woman but her bathroom is actually rather more modest than

Banquets are a routine part of royal life. While resting one's arm on the back of a royal chair is against protocol, Princess Diana doesn't seem to mind.

those of many of her subjects. A white enamel bath, which has seen better days, white floor tiles covered with an ancient oilcloth and a white plastic loo seat is the prosaic answer to this popular fantasy of royal life. She does not even have a shower – but does run to a heated towel rail.

Her bedroom, which adjoins the Duke of Edinburgh's dressing room and overlooks Constitution Hill, is equally plain. Of course there is a queen-sized bed, a cupola of blue silk above her headboard which matches the carpet and wallpaper. Traditional white cotton sheets and blankets – rather than a modern duvet – cover her bed. Even in the height of summer a red furry hot-water bottle is placed in her bed to take the chill off. The palace is a notoriously draughty place.

However this simplicity is deceptive. The Queen has four dressers, two pages, and at least three footmen to fuss over her. Each morning her dresser runs her bath, lays out her clothes in the dressing room which adjoins the bathroom, takes in the quaintly named 'calling tray' of percolated coffee – a special blend is supplied by Harrods – and pulls back the curtains. The Queen is happy if it is foggy and wet because it means Prince Philip will be unable to fly from the palace gardens in a red Wessex helicopter. Unlike her husband, she has a morbid dislike of this mode of transport.

While the Queen is dressing, her liveried footman is attending to her nine corgis and dorgies, who sleep in a boxroom opposite the Audience Chamber. The room itself is a jumble of favoured wicker baskets, cushions and canvas-covered chairs – hardly the doggie equivalent of a five star hotel. Their food is nothing special either: a diet of tinned dog meat mixed with wheat and barley biscuits ladled into plastic bowls with an old spoon and laid on a green plastic sheet in the King's Corridor.

The Queen, who has had corgis ever since she was given Dookie, a Pembrokeshire, for her sixth birthday, knows from painful experience that they are not as cuddly as they look. During a pre-luncheon conversation with headmistress Joy Pinder and crime writer P. D. James, one of her

Princess Diana manages to coax Prince Charles on to the dance floor. He prefers chat to cha-cha.

dogs ran up to her and bit her ankle. 'Talk about biting the hand that feeds you,' commented the Queen drily before going on to explain that as herding dogs this was their natural instinct.

It does not stop her feeding them breadsticks under the dining table at mealtimes or allowing them into her study when she is working on her interminable red boxes. 'She is far more demonstrative with them than she is with her own family,' says one friend of the royal family.

They are certainly quieter than George V's parrot which unnerved visitors with its squawking and rather less cosseted than Edward VII's terrier Caesar who had his own footman that followed him everywhere he went. When the Queen is dressed – around 8.15 a.m. – the footman lets her corgis into the study where she often works on her official papers or personal correspondence for half an hour before a breakfast of toast and scrambled egg – or eggs Benedict if the Queen wishes to indulge herself with one of her favourite dishes.

When Prince Philip is in residence he joins the Queen in her private dining room next to her study. On each 20 November, the anniversary of the royal wedding, there are always flowers waiting on the breakfast table – a remembrance gift from Philip. Normally her flowers (favourites are long-stemmed pink carnations from the Sandringham greenhouses) are arranged by her page Christopher Bray.

Prince Philip's tastes – his regular morning diet is live yoghurt from the Windsor dairy, bran and hot water mixed into a breakfast cup – make the Queen seem positively decadent. As a pupil of the German philosopher Kurt Hahn, he puts little value on material possessions. His mother Princess Andrew, who started her own religious order when she lived at the palace, was otherworldly – apart from her addiction to nicotine. His rooms have an ascetic simplicity, decorated with his own bold oil paintings, cartoons, family portraits and electronic gadgetry.

While Prince Philip has a computer installed on his desk, the Queen has no space for such electronic aids. Her desk is huge, laden with family photographs in silver frames, a silver tray containing her pens, acres of paperwork and white blotting paper.

However affairs of the heart take precedence over affairs of state. The Queen, who enjoys keeping up with the latest palace gossip, is sometimes seen, her red boxes forgotten for the moment, listening to a footman giving her the Downstairs news. On one occasion a servant, newly arrived at the palace, stopped in his tracks when he saw footman John Davis, a loquacious Welshman, standing at the Queen's study door chatting away merrily about the plight of a housemaid. He recalls, 'he was talking to the Queen as though she were a neighbour on the other side of a fence. Yet the Queen didn't seem to mind at all. She was fascinated by chitchat.'

However it is only those servants she knows well who can get away with this kind of conversation. Nervous new arrivals are apt to disturb the regal calm. Designer David Sassoon, now a favourite of the Princess of Wales, remembers his own anxiety when, as an apprentice dressmaker, he was asked to fit young Princess Anne for a bridesmaid's dress.

The fitting, which took place in the Queen's dressing room, went well until the Queen arrived. Sassoon, all fingers and thumbs, bowed and shuffled backwards. Unfortunately he put his foot in a bowl of water for the corgis, sending it spraying

The Queen and the Duchess of York enjoy an evening at a hit West End play.

everywhere. The Queen murmured her approval of the dress and then asked drily, 'Will it wash?'

Once a designer, like a servant, has fitted in and become part of the social furniture, the Queen likes hearing their anecdotes. One she particularly enjoyed concerned a tiresome aristocrat she knew who insisted on having a beaded flapper-style dress made for her. It took three weeks of painstaking sewing to complete. At the final fitting she asked her designer, 'Is it washable?' 'Madame,' he replied tartly, 'it isn't even wearable!'

On one occasion designer Ian Thomas arrived to find the Queen on her hands and knees picking up dress pins. Naturally Thomas, who has been with her for some twenty years and shares an interest in horses, bounded to her assistance. That Christmas he gave her a red horseshoe magnet decorated with silk ribbon. Delighted with such an apposite gift, the Queen had her own surprise in store.

The next time he visited, the Queen asked him to go into the King's Corridor where a present was waiting. As he wondered what was in store, the Sovereign, who does not have a reputation for extravagance, gestured towards an Old Master hanging on the wall. For a moment he was taken aback until he saw the real object of her largesse – a dog basket containing a delightful corgi puppy called Frisky.

Indeed a flurry – staff call it a puddle – of barking, yapping corgis accompany the Queen on all her peregrinations around the palace. 'It's like standing on a moving carpet,' jokes Princess Diana when she brings William and Harry for tea in the soothing pastel-green dining room.

This afternoon ritual, a hangover from Edwardian days, gives the Queen the chance to see her royal relatives informally. Royal courtiers now concede that when the Prince and Princess of Wales had marriage difficulties in 1987 they visited the Queen to discuss their troubles over a cup of tea. Over the years much finessing of family business has taken place under the shadow of Pieter de Hooch's Dutch masterpiece *The Cardplayer* as guests choose from home-made chocolate cake, and cheese and cucumber sandwiches. The Queen likes to play mother and make the tea herself even though it is her staff who have done all the preparation. She simply presses the red switch

In a rather posed portrait the Queen Mother listens to her daughters playing a tune.

THAT'S ENTERTAINMENT

Theatre and costume are at the heart of the pomp and circumstance that is the Crown. Indeed royalty is the original street theatre, the brilliant processions and stunning pageants the lifeblood of monarchy. While Prince Edward hit the headlines when he decided to make a career as a theatrical producer, he was no more than following in a private family tradition. These days he even holds meetings in his rooms at Buckingham Palace to plan new ventures. Princess Elizabeth was a star of the Christmas pantomimes while it is always said that Princess Margaret could have made a career in showbusiness.

Former palace valet John Hutchinson recalls, 'She would play a Chopin or Strauss waltz better than many professional painists. She is a wonderful mimic too. One time George VI could not help bursting into laughter even while he scolded her, for pantomiming a noble peer who had just departed.' She is not the only Windsor with ability. Prince Charles is a talented actor and magician while Princess Diana and the Duchess of York fooled everyone when they dressed up as policewomen on Prince Andrew's stag night.

on her Russell Hobbs kettle and mashes the tea.

Lord Mountbatten was famous for breezing into the palace to see his elder sister Princess Alice, who lived out her last years there, or to take tea with the Sovereign. Topics ranged from Prince Charles's girlfriends, changing the family name to Mountbatten Windsor, the Civil List and, portentously, a bodyguard for Uncle Dickie himself. James Mooney Boyle, a former Mountbatten aide, recalls, 'Dickie told the Queen, "Who would want to bother with an old man like me?" Ironic really in view of his assassination in Ireland.'

The Queen, who took a wry view of Mountbatten's bombastic manner, only lost patience with this self-appointed shop steward of royalty on a chilly March afternoon when they were discussing Prince Michael's love for a divorced Catholic, Marie-Christine von Riebnitz. Mountbatten pushed her suit, the Queen vigorously pointed out the problems of allowing a Catholic divorcee into the family – especially as her own sister, Princess Margaret was prevented from marrying a divorcee, Group Captain Peter Townsend.

The argument raged on and for once the Queen lost her customary cool demeanour. As Mountbatten left she followed him to the top of the stairs, shouting, 'You're wrong, you're wrong,' as he bounded out of the palace. His former private secretary John Barratt says that Mountbatten warned the Sovereign that Prince Michael proposed to live with the Czech-born aristocrat unless the Queen gave way. A measure of Mountbatten's skill and the Queen's forgiving nature was that the newly weds were granted a grace and favour home at Kensington Palace.

While teatime is a domestic interlude, the pressing day-to-day business of monarchy means that the Queen has to keep in touch with her family and friends by telephone. She has phones in every room, as well as four on her desk which include a direct line to Downing Street, an internal phone and a scrambled line for personal calls.

Her racing manager Earl Carnarvon expects regular calls from her, especially during the flat racing season. 'I speak to the Queen in the evening about the next day's racing and future plans,' he says. 'She is an exceptionally good judge of a race.'

The Duchess of York has a wide circle of showbiz and American friends who have invested palace parties with glamour and flair. She often invites her pals to her apartment for an impromptu supper.

Nevertheless her ambition of winning the Derby has so far eluded her. As one of her closest friends – his country seat, Highclere House, is a favoured royal retreat – the Earl frequently dines with her, acting as a trusted conduit for news from the world outside the palace walls.

Naturally she keeps in close contact with the Queen Mother who lives along The Mall at Clarence House. As the Queen once remarked, 'Although we may have our own opinions it is almost completely true that what mother thinks today, tomorrow I find out.'

These regular morning chats have given rise to the myth that when the Queen telephones the Queen Mother at Clarence House, the operator says, 'Your Majesty, Her Majesty, Your Majesty.' In fact the calls are scrambled.

When the Queen Mother is invited to dinner at Buckingham Palace, her daughter knows that she is such a notoriously bad timekeeper that she makes a point of pretending that dinner will be served half an hour before its actual time. No matter, she still contrives to arrive late.

As she sips her daily glass of champagne the Queen Mother, who is, in the words of her private secretary, 'a great enjoyer', likes to tease her daughter about her relatively frugal lifestyle. When the Queen pondered the question of treating herself to a glass of wine, her mother said archly, 'Is that wise? You know you have to reign all afternoon.' The Queen does have her little indulgences. Salad tossed in mayonnaise (she dislikes vinaigrette), *crème brûlée*, Sandringham-grown oranges soaked in cognac, and Bendicks mints get the regal seal of approval.

She is also superstitious and has been known to surprise her guests by throwing spilt salt over her shoulder. It is a family characteristic. Palace valets were forbidden to turn over Edward VII's mattress on a Friday and he refused to sit down to dinner when there were thirteen seated around the table.

The Queen's dinner parties are more intimate but no less regal. King Constantine of Greece – 'Tino' to his friends – often travels from his home in Hampstead Garden Suburb for supper. King Juan Carlos of Spain and King Hussein of Jordan, who agreed to let the Duke and Duchess of York use his country mansion while their own home was under construction, also enjoy the Sovereign's hospitality when they are in town.

If she fancies an evening out it is the job of her equerry to recommend suitable shows. A leading

Lord Mountbatten often visited the palace for tea with the Queen. They had a heated discussion when he pursued the issue of Prince Michael's wish to marry Princess Michael, a Catholic divorcee.

theatrical ticket agency holds seats at various West End theatres in case Buckingham Palace should signal an impromptu visit. The Queen and the Duchess of York enjoyed a private evening together at a performance of the hit play *Lettice and Lovage* while the Queen's friends are quick to check on new dramas that impress the critics.

If she is invited to dine with friends like Lord and Lady Weinstock or Princess Alexandra and Sir Angus Ogilvy there is no such thing as a 'quiet evening out'. Every time she leaves the palace a gaggle of courtiers gathers to wave her off while her detectives signal to police control that 'Purple One', the Queen's call sign, is on the move.

There is an assumption too of punctuality by host and regal guest – which is why even comedian Barry Humphries was taken aback when he shouted, 'Who the bloody hell is it?', to discover Prince Charles waiting on the doorstep of his Hampstead home. The Prince had arrived early.

Even if the Queen decides to commune with the television for the evening, there is a certain formality about the occasion. A favourite light supper of chicken and salad is served by a liveried footman and eaten with solid-silver cutlery underneath a crystal chandelier. The Queen enjoys too the privilege of video tapes of television shows delivered to the palace by the BBC – although that didn't prevent her television set from breaking down just as Neil Armstrong prepared to step on to the moon.

Her preferences range from horsey programmes to light comedies such as 'Only Fools and Horses' and mysteries like P. D. James's 'Devices and Desires'. However her taste in televised violence extends only so far as wrestling, which she describes as 'tremendous fun'. It is unlikely that she would approve of Prince William's fascination for Sylvester Stallone's bloodcurdling Rambo and Rocky films ordered from his local video store.

A well-written biography, *The Times* crossword puzzle or an hour poring over her unending paperwork are the Queen's preferred alternatives to television. When she retires at around eleven o'clock a uniformed policeman, wearing a pair of carpet slippers, takes his position on a settee in the King's Corridor outside her bedroom. While the Queen and her family may live in 'splendid isolation' they are never truly alone.

III

UPSTAIRS DOWNSTAIRS

*T*irst impressions are misleading. The casual visitor passing the two uniformed policemen and entering the staff door at the side of Buckingham Palace could be forgiven for thinking that they were in any ministry building in Whitehall.

The serried rows of red, yellow and blue work cards, the unblinking gaze of the wall-mounted camera, the array of cheap dun-coloured chairs and the steady flow of staff who pass through with a nod in the direction of the duty clerk behind his desk all contribute to a nondescript atmosphere.

A reusable manila envelope addressed to the Royal Dairy at Windsor is the first clue. There are more when the amber light on the double security doors turns to green to allow visitors into the courtyard. The porter in his distinctive blue overalls, with the EIIR cypher woven on to the lapels, throwing offcuts of red carpet into a skip, the forlorn ranks of lime-green sentry boxes and the mountain of black boxes fastened with leather straps and marked 'Private Secretary The Queen' give the game away.

While most visitors to Buckingham Palace use the Privy Purse Door which is on the right of the public frontage, it is the staff and goods entrance

The family firm gathers to celebrate the Duke and Duchess of York's wedding. For once demarcation lines are forgotten as Downstairs staff stand with royalty. But there's always the Rolls to clean.

which is the real hub of activity. Its workings are proof that the palace never sleeps.

It is three o'clock in the morning and all's well. Even as a guardsman takes an illicit drag on his cigarette while he patrols the gravel courtyard, a Sherpa van from Express Dairies is nosing its way inside the palace, carefully carrying two metal churns of milk and a box of cheese from the Windsor dairy for the Queen's personal use. It has been said that Her Majesty was only convinced she was Queen when in 1952 she first saw her cypher on the royal milk bottles with their specially printed sides and gold tops showing her monogram.

During the day an endless supply of biscuits, bread, fruit, fish and other goods is delivered to help to keep the machinery of monarchy turning.

Buckingham Palace may seem like a well-run hotel or a civil service department, but try telling that to PC 297 Tom Wallington celebrating his retirement after 31 unbroken years as the side door police officer. He walks into the staff bar grinning broadly and proudly clutching a signed photograph of the Queen. Five minutes earlier he had nervously fingered his tie before being ushered into the presence. 'Don't worry,' Lady Susan Hussey, herself 25 years a lady-in-waiting to the Queen, told him with a friendly smile. 'It's always different meeting the Queen as an individual rather than in uniform. She understands.'

Priceless gold and silver plate, kept in an underground vault, is cleaned by staff under the vigilant supervision of the Yeoman of the Gold Plate.

When the speeches in the crowded bar are over, the ruddy-faced Devonian raises his glass. 'It wouldn't be right to finish without a toast to our governor – the Queen,' he says with the enthusiasm of a man still walking on air after his royal audience.

Paternalistic, chauvinistic, obstructive and inefficient – 'Your staff have cocked it up again,' Lord Mountbatten told Prince Charles with cheerful regularity – the Firm nevertheless commands a loyalty and devotion no civil service department or hotel enjoys. While staff grumble about the constant demands of the Duchess of York – 'Roll on the revolution,' complains a footman as he flops in an easy chair in the staff room after one exasperating encounter – it is the small but authoritative figure of the Queen who makes the knees go weak, the heart flutter and eyes moisten with an unswerving romantic allegiance to the Crown.

'We're all family here,' explains Cyril Dickman, for 40 years the palace steward. Since his retirement he lives in a Duchy of Cornwall grace and favour house – a reward for a lifetime's loyal service – but still likes to drop in to the palace for a drink and to reminisce about the old days when servants had to powder their hair. 'We've got a tin of that dreadful stuff somewhere,' he jokes.

He and his two brothers – who still work for the Queen – set up something of a record by marrying three sisters, the Hamilton girls from Scotland, who also worked at the palace. Many others have found companionship, happiness and love under the palace roof – although married women are not allowed to remain in royal service. As with any community there is a darker side. There have been tragic suicides, tales of male prostitution – allegations subsequently documented by Conservative MP Geoffrey Dickens – and criminal behaviour. A footman woke up in his palace room one morning to discover that his next-door neighbour had stored boxes of gelignite in his bedroom.

A consistent complaint is loneliness. For a young footman or housemaid, often in their first job away from home, the palace can seem a friendless place. Even a young girl waiting to become a princess has her problems. In the days before her wedding Lady Diana Spencer wandered along the corridors, a Sony Walkman stereo clamped to her head, exploring the endless rooms. Tap-dancing lessons in the Throne Room under the supervision of her dance teacher Lily Snipp were a welcome diversion but beneath the excitement of the wedding build-up she felt rather lost.

Princess Grace of Monaco noticed the uncertainty in Diana when she met her at a reception at the American embassy just before the wedding. Ignoring the other guests who were still buzzing over Diana's choice of a daring black gown with its plunging neckline, Princess Grace whisked her off to the powder room. Diana poured her heart out about the publicity, her sense of isolation and fears about what the future held. 'Don't worry,' Princess Grace consoled. 'It will get a lot worse.'

Lady Diana, discouraged from spending too much time chatting to staff, couldn't even drown her sorrows in the staff bar. With its regimental plaques and club prices, it is the time-honoured gathering place.

The Welsh rugby team used to call in for a pint before a match at Twickenham, while Prince Andrew danced the night away at one of the bar's discos. There are numerous sports clubs but the swimming pool is out of bounds ever since a footman was caught urinating from the diving board.

Entertainers Bruce Forsyth and Roy Castle have been hired by the Royal Household Social Club to amuse staff while most evenings, starting at 7.30 p.m., the cosy private cinema screens the latest release, with drinks next door during the interval. Apart from a friendly visit by the Duke and Duchess of Gloucester each Christmas the royal family rarely patronizes the palace's 'Palais'. 'After dinner there aren't too many films appropriate for showing guests besides Walt Disney,' explains Princess Anne. The days when Winston Churchill sat with King George VI and Queen Elizabeth watching black and white Hollywood offerings are long gone.

Going too is the automatic assumption that new arrivals to the palace will stay for a lifetime. While royal service can bring security, privilege and friendship, the poor pay and long hours soon pall. 'Underpaid and undervalued' is the notice on the staff Civil Service Union noticeboard and the rapid turnover in some departments in recent years is a signal that these days youngsters are prepared to vote with their feet.

In spite of the glamorous address, recruits soon find that polishing silver and washing up is the same in the Queen's employ as elsewhere. The spartan rooms have changed little since George V's days when 'calling boys' brought hot water up three flights of steps.

Indeed the inevitable tightening of palace security and the historical erosion of the service ethos in British society has dramatically affected working relations between the royal family and their staff. While the royal family is implicitly respected, their courtiers can no longer take that deference for granted. Footmen who are prepared to go through the tricky ritual of laying down the morning calling tray in the dark for a prince do not feel that same obligation for an equerry, who is after all a civil servant just like them. It especially rankled when one equerry complained to the palace steward that his footman had forgotten to tune his bedside radio to BBC's 'Today' show.

Hand in hand with that respect went a feeling of mutual trust, a social lubricant that oiled the palace machine. No longer. When Princess Anne became the first member of the royal family in

history to be fingerprinted in the criminal investigation to find the thief who took her letters, it marked a tragic turning point. While the palace culprit has never been discovered, the episode has soured for ever the bond between the royal family and those who serve them. Indeed when servants are present, members of the royal family, in particular Prince Philip and Prince and Princess Michael of Kent, have been known to speak German when they wish to discuss matters of a confidential nature.

However only a handful of Downstairs staff ever come into personal contact with the royal family. The Christmas party is one of the few opportunities for staff to see the Queen, Princess Diana and the others close up.

This party is usually held on the Tuesday or Thursday before the Queen leaves for Sandringham. However staff only receive an invitation, issued by the master of the Household, every other year. Even the ballroom would be too congested if every member of staff and their guests were asked at the same time.

It is a night of riotous revelry, at times bordering on the bacchanalian. The evenings start decorously

The Queen, here with former American president Gerald Ford, signals to the bandleader to slow the music down when she takes to the floor.

enough with staff in black tie, long dresses and long-service medals dancing to live music.

One long-serving member of staff described these occasions in the following terms: 'They used to be quite lavish affairs. Now due to cutbacks only wine, beer and soft drinks are served. Spirits were stopped a few years ago after one party. That's because so many staff were so drunk that they had to be carted off by ambulance. I remember staff, especially older ones, lying insensible on the chaise-longues and other furniture in the state rooms. What a night that was!

'Normally the royal family arrive after dinner at around nine-thirty. They are dressed in their tiaras and other regalia and proceed to wander around the semi-drunken rabble. Staff push and kick to get to the front to see if they are recognized or spoken to so that they can impress the others. The royal family always have one dance before leaving for their private apartments for a drink and a good gossip about their servants. Staff leave walking or otherwise around one in the morning.'

In fact the Queen has even abandoned her annual dance with a member of staff, usually a young footman. Officially it is so that she can mix with more people. Unofficially it is to save the wear and tear on her toes from clumsy and apprehensive staff. When the Sovereign is about to take

A postillion enjoys a break before donning his hat, which fits neatly over his half wig. Prince Philip stopped the tradition of powdering wigs.

the floor for a twirl the bandleader is given a discreet signal to slow down the tempo so that the Queen's feet and evening gown remain intact.

Her caution is understandable. 'I apologize again most humbly for having stepped on your train of your dress and torn the hem,' wrote a contrite Esmond Butler, the Queen's former assistant press secretary, after one dance turned to disaster. He continued, 'I feel I should have made some gesture such as offering to sew it up for you (I used to be a Boy Scout and a sailor) but perhaps you have someone slightly more competent. In any case I am very sorry. It was such a beautiful dress.'

The morning after the night before, the Queen and the rest of the family eagerly await gossip about the behaviour of their staff. It is delivered by a hand-picked group of servants whose titles belie their influence. They are the valets, dressers, detectives and royal pages whose constant proximity to royalty can subtly transform the relationship from master-servant to trusted confidante, confessor or even at times surrogate parent.

The Queen herself has no shortage of Downstairs staff to call on who serve up everything from breakfast to juicy titbits of gossip. She has two Pages of the Back Stairs, Christopher Bray and Paul Whybrew, whose title describes the confidential nature of their job. In the old days their duty was to escort the lovers of the king or queen up the back stairs and then remain silent. Today they are at the top of the palace pecking order and act as go-betweens for other staff who wish to approach the monarch.

The Queen also has four dressers including Peggy Hoath and May Prentice who both worked for Hartnell and a newer arrival, Brenda Williams. It is their job to care for the endless variety of day and evening clothes which make up what Georgina Howell called 'a unique, almost abstract and mystical wardrobe: uniforms, decorations, overdressing, pomp, allusions and references'. In days gone by the job of dressing the monarch was performed by two noble ladies. The Woman of the Bedchamber handed the queen's clothes to the Lady of the Bedchamber who in turn passed them to the queen. These more streamlined times have resulted in a closed corps of dressers who care for the Queen as well as her clothes and jewellery.

The official 'number one' dresser is so influential that staff refer to her respectfully as 'Queen Elizabeth Mark II'. This diminutive Svengali to the Sovereign comes from an unlikely background. Miss Margaret MacDonald, the daughter of a Scottish railway worker, has been by the Queen's side since she was barely able to speak. Now 86, Bobo – as she is known to the royal family – retains a formidable authority in spite of her physical frailty.

'She is my right hand,' says the Queen of her longest-serving retainer and turns a blind eye to the half-bottle of champagne Bobo enjoys with her evening meal. The Queen's affection and loyalty is understandable. From childhood, her constant companion was Bobo. They shared the same bedroom and when the air-raid sirens sounded during the war it was Bobo who hurried Princesses Elizabeth and Margaret into the air-raid shelter at Windsor Castle and stayed with them until the all clear sounded.

Until recently she was the first person the Queen saw each morning, the woman who controlled her wardrobe and influenced many of her opinions. She takes a dim view of the 'flippant' young royal generation like the Princess of Wales and the Duchess of York, has little time for Prince Philip, Princess Margaret or Princess Anne, considering them 'rebels', but dotes on Prince Charles. Nor is she afraid to voice those views. She soundly ticked off Princess Anne when she failed to return one of the Queen's tiaras which she had borrowed for a photographic session in the palace. After searching the Princess's apartment, Bobo was horrified to discover that the diamond tiara had been casually thrown under the royal bed.

Plain-speaking, sharp-tongued but with a robust sense of humour, Miss MacDonald has never married. Her first and only loves have been the Crown – and the Queen. She has no interests or life outside the palace. On one occasion the Queen ordered the royal yacht *Britannia* to anchor off Invergordon during the traditional Western Isles cruise so that Bobo could see her sister Ruby, formerly Princess Margaret's dresser. However Bobo decided to stay on board. She didn't want to leave the woman she has served for 60 years.

It is no coincidence that her hairstyle, her clothes specially made by Hartnell and her mannerisms are identical to those of her royal mistress. Or is it the other way round? The Queen's hairdresser Charles Martin coifs Bobo's hair in her second-floor apartment, conveniently near the Queen's lift, as soon as he has finished with the monarch, and Queen Mark II is served her tea and biscuits immediately after the Sovereign. 'She has total influence over the Queen,' says a friend who has known Miss MacDonald for 25 years. 'She is a great friend to Her Majesty, perhaps the only true friend outside her family that she possesses.' Indeed the Queen is at something of a loss when she is absent. On one occasion she was visiting Highclere House when Bobo fell ill. As there was no-one around to perform the usual role of a dresser – running the bath, laying out clothes, taking messages – the Queen simply could not function. She sat on the edge of her bed waiting for a replacement dresser to arrive from Buckingham Palace under police escort.

This regal institutionalization is not confined to the Queen. Prince Charles too found it difficult to co-ordinate the bath taps when his valet fell ill on another weekend away from the palace. As one member of staff explained, 'It may sound strange but you have to see it from their perspective. They are groomed to talk to prime ministers or ambassadors and appear constantly on parade. Most of us would come apart at the seams if we were put in their position but they sail through. Similarly when the royal machine breaks down they are at a loss.'

Just before Christmas 1990 the Queen made a private visit to London's King Edward VII's Hospital for Officers where Bobo was recovering after breaking her leg in a fall. She had intended to stay in for Christmas but the Queen was bereft without her eyes and ears. Bobo was persuaded to return to the palace and she has since enjoyed round-the-clock nursing supervision – paid for by the Queen.

A constant stream of visitors to her second-floor rooms means that she is perhaps better informed than at any time for years. This is no idle boast. On one occasion several porters were moving a huge oil of Charles I from the Picture Gallery when a colleague marched by carrying an aluminium ladder. As in all the best movies, the inevitable happened. The ladder went through the canvas tearing a six-inch gash in the precious Van Dyck. Once more the branches of the palace grapevine soon heard the cries of disaster. The Queen was told even before the Surveyor of the Queen's Pictures.

Again when a footman was taken seriously ill near the ground-floor lift late one night, the monarch was aware of the incident even before the ambulance arrived. A servant on the scene told Bobo who quickly relayed the information to the Queen. There is self-interest at work. As most staff never speak directly to the royal family, a chat with Miss MacDonald does little harm to their chances of promotion.

It is therefore ironic that Miss MacDonald must address all officials and members of the Household, those courtiers technically her superior, as 'sir' or 'madam' in accordance with correct etiquette. Yet when she utters the phrase 'I will have to speak to the Queen about that' in her soft Scottish brogue, it can send a chill through the most urbane administrator.

None the less if the palace is anything, it is a place where position counts more than personality. Its structure is a lethal administrative cocktail which combines the arcane traditions of an old-established military regiment, the feudal customs of an aristocratic estate spiced with the civil service rulebook. The television company troubleshooter Sir John Harvey-Jones might relish the challenge of changing the old guard at Buckingham Palace but he would have a long campaign on his hands. Even the doughty Miss MacDonald had to fight hard when she took on the system in a long-running dispute over meals.

She complained bitterly when she discovered that her rival, nanny Mabel Anderson, enjoyed a form of room service in the nursery even when the royal children were not in residence. Bobo felt that her status entitled her to similar treatment. The palace authorities quoted custom and practice – all dressers eat in the stewards' room – but she would have none of it. This wrangle went on for months until the Queen was forced to intervene to keep the peace. Bobo got her way. Since that confrontation every meal is carried from the stewards' room to her private apartment by a liveried footman.

Normally staff are allocated to one of five different dining rooms. While the days may be over

when 'upper servants' sat down to a free four-course meal with white wine and sherry, dining room service is still linked to palace status.

At the apex of this Gothic fancy are the members of the Household. It is one of the world's most exclusive clubs. While there is no joining fee or application form, members are allowed in by invitation only – and that invitation comes from the Queen. These are the private secretaries, comptrollers and assistants who hold positions roughly equivalent to senior directors of commercial companies. Most are from public schools, usually Eton or Harrow, or the more fashionable regiments. Britain's female population and ethnic minorities are as well represented as the nation's business community. That is not at all.

If Queen Victoria were to review the composition of the present Household she would find comfort in its familiarity. At Court the faces may have changed but the names remain the same. The Norfolks, the Airlies, the Cholmondeleys, the Northumberlands and the Westmorlands form the nucleus of a royal Household which is firmly rooted in the shires and the old aristocracy. When Prince Charles's private secretary Edward Adeane abruptly resigned he ended a tradition that has seen three generations of his family guide and advise the monarchy.

Their grand dining arrangements reflect their status as the nation's premier old boys' club. Members forgather in the equerries' room for a drink before lunch. The meal is served in the Household dining room, a grand room lit by three chandeliers and with French windows overlooking the garden terrace. The patterned Indian carpet was made to Queen Mary's orders to harmonize with the light green walls and gold frieze. Their menu is written in French and the Master of the Household has a silver bell by his side to summon staff. In the old days there was no need. The dozen or so diners are waited on by two footmen together with pages and a wine butler.

Senior officials – the royal version of line managers who look after administrative and clerical details – enjoy the delights of the Lady Barrington Room while secretaries have to walk from their offices to the officials' dining room in the south wing.

THE PALACE THAT NEVER SLEEPS

Buckingham Palace is always open for business. It is guarded around the clock by armed police and soldiers while deliveries start long before daybreak. The milk, yoghurt and cheese from the Windsor dairy arrives at 3.00 a.m. and the post about two hours later. By 6.30 a.m. as the housemaids are vacuuming the miles of red carpet, J. Lyons & Co. are delivering racks of croissants and bread to the ground-floor kitchens. While the days when virtually all the royal staff lived in are now over, a significant number have their own rooms ensuring that the palace continues to be a thriving village.

Throughout the day there is a steady stream of callers to the tradesmen's entrance at the palace. Before Princess Diana has finished her morning swim, trays of meat pies, boxes of biscuits and assorted parcels have been delivered. Company associations with royalty go back a long way. For example the royal warrant holders McVitie & Price, endeared themselves to the royal family by baking the wedding cakes for Queen Mary, the Queen Mother and the Queen.

6.40 a.m.: Cartons of Barradale Farm eggs are delivered. 6.45 a.m.: Fishmongers H. S. Linwood & Sons arrive. 'If it swims and the Queen wants it, we get it.'
9.00 a.m.: A bouquet of expensive roses comes from Harrods.
10.30 a.m.: Lifeguards disembark for ceremonial duties.

Both the officials' and the next-door stewards' dining rooms have the air of a dowdy seaside boarding house circa 1950. The dull cream walls, starched white linen and dull utility furniture give the inevitable impression of menus consisting of brown Windsor soup and overcooked roast beef, and the expectation of a pervading smell of boiled cabbage. In fact the palace fare is well above average. As the palace chef is the second highest paid staff member with a salary of £20,000 ($36,000) a year it is not surprising that high-calibre chefs have been attracted to the gleaming kitchens.

Generations of clerks, valets and pages have passed the dusty display of alabaster statuary, the oil painting of a beefeater by Malcolm Stewart and a glass case filled with polished copper Victorian kitchen utensils on their way to these dining rooms. In the stewards' dining room, used by the elite of the Downstairs staff – the pages of the back stairs, dressers and valets – times have moved on a little since the days when servants sat down for meals in strict order of precedence.

Before the meal they used to stand behind their chairs waiting for the palace steward to say grace. No one could leave until the steward had recited a closing grace followed by toasts, drunk in water, to the Queen. When this ritual was completed the Queen's dresser led the way out of the room, followed by the others in order of rank. Now it is more like a self-service restaurant, as is the staff canteen where the rest of the domestic staff, which includes around 45 catering staff and 58 housemaids together with about 50 footmen, butlers and other male staff, gather for their meals.

Outsiders present a problem. A parlour game for royal equerries is to try and assign those in the business or police world a suitable grade which relates to the palace hierarchy. Bowler-hatted Superintendent Albert Perkins, the Queen's former bodyguard, was always concerned to see that his officers were given the treatment due their rank. The head of the royal protection squad, who holds the rank of assistant commissioner, is allowed to dine with the Household, while back-up officers eat in the stewards' room. This attention to position is not unique to the palace. When Prince Charles was serving in the Royal Navy, his Scotland Yard bodyguard John Maclean was

The ornate Music Room where Princess Diana learned to tap-dance when she lived at the palace.

barred from the officers' mess because he did not have the required rank.

As one member of staff says, 'The palace is full of rigid rules which outsiders find difficult to comprehend. Every nuance of behaviour is silently acknowledged. The Queen would no more wander into her page's vestibule across the corridor from her study than her housemaid would dream of entering her apartments without the approval of the Queen's page. That is accepted practice.'

Custom dictates that dressers and valets are allowed to use the front gate rather than the staff door. Scotland Yard bodyguards and pages of the back stairs are referred to by their surnames whereas the rest of the Downstairs staff are called by their Christian names.

Little wonder that when the Duke of Edinburgh's valet John Dean arrived at the palace from Clarence House he found the atmosphere 'most fussy and fastidious'. Elderly housemaids bowed their way out of his presence, conscious that if their duties were not completed by noon they could be in trouble.

On the stroke of midday the former lord chamberlain, the Earl of Scarborough, used to leave his offices in St James's Palace to inspect progress at Buckingham Palace. Maids who were still working hid behind curtains or cupboards rather than face his displeasure. A standing instruction was that they should make themselves scarce when royalty was around. As she was walking along a corridor Queen Mary once spotted a maid dive into a cubby-hole. The Queen opened the door and told her it was permissible to come out.

Even today housemaids are only officially allowed to see the royal family on the night of a state banquet when they put on their best uniforms and long-service medals of the Royal Victorian Order and stand quietly in the corridors to watch the parade of tiaras and regal finery.

These cherished Royal Victorian medals, which are in the Queen's personal gift, are a source of both pride and rancour. Their distribution epitomizes the intricate distinctions of status and class. The order, founded in 1896 by Queen Victoria because she felt that politicians were having too much say in the award of honours, has five classes, the top two carrying knighthoods.

The Royal Victorian Medal, the lowest class of decoration, is given to staff and stewards after 25 years' service. However after just five years officials and senior officials are eligible for the class above, Member of the Victorian Order. Naturally members of the Household are made knights or companions of the order.

When the Queen goes abroad orders are distributed with quite lavish generosity – much to the annoyance of long-serving staff at Buckingham Palace. With good reason. For a few days' hard work on, say, a tour by the Princess of Wales, an embassy official can be presented with a medal which staff at royal headquarters achieve only after years of dedicated service.

Those who read the runes in these things can distinguish in the niceties of the various grades of award the esteem with which the individual is held by the Queen. So for example it was noted that the Queen's former equerry Commander Timothy Laurence, the author of the stolen letters to Princess Anne, was only made a member of the Victorian Order. Normally outgoing equerries are given a high grade, that of lieutenant. A possible sign of the Queen's displeasure that his secret and

affectionate relationship had been made public?

Similarly the historian Hugo Vickers believes that the Queen may have known that Anthony Blunt, the distinguished Surveyor of the Queen's Pictures, was a Communist spy before he was finally unmasked. A likely clue is that on his retirement he was not invested with the usual GCVO (Grand Cross Royal Victorian Order). Indeed reading the palace tea-leaves, Earl Grey of course, is an art practised by historians and writers in the same way as foreign diplomats analyzed the nuances of every statement from the Kremlin in order to divine shifts in Russian policy.

As the head office of the House of Windsor, Buckingham Palace maintains a façade of imperturbable continuity, a still centre in a changing universe. It may be a wheezing, clanking steam engine in a silicon-chip society but, as the *Boston Globe* said after the royal wedding, the monarchy still manages to 'pull off ceremonies the way the army of Israel pulls off commando raids'.

This royal train is kept on the tracks by the Downstairs staff who ensure the Queen's dignity and comfort while the Upstairs courtiers watch out for danger signals ahead. Just as the dressers and valets keep the Queen in touch within the palace walls, so the private secretary and his assistants patrol the corridors of power to protect the monarch's position.

The rapier rather than the bludgeon is their chosen weapon. It is wielded with such elaborate courtesy and good manners that victims rarely feel a twinge – until it is too late. Indeed urbane civility is the byword in the palace as Basil Boothroyd, Prince Philip's official biographer, discovered when he bumped into the Queen's then private secretary Sir Michael Adeane. As he politely passed the time of day he got the distinct impression that he was detaining one of Britain's most influential men rather against his will. It was another couple of minutes, however, before Adeane excused himself with profuse apologies. 'I do hope you will forgive me, but I've just heard that my house is on fire. I wouldn't mind but it's part of St James's Palace.'

Even a courtier's smooth demeanour can be ruffled working for the family firm. This phrase may conjure up images of a structure in which the

Queen acts as chairman of the board, issuing dictats and decrees to the rest of the royal directors who are accountable to the nation as shareholders. In fact the royal family is more akin to a loose federation of independent royal households with little central direction or control. As one senior member of the royal Household says, 'We are very decentralized. No sensible businessman would allow so much autonomy or allow the organization to run without overall control. We live in very watertight compartments and you would be amazed at the lack of co-operation between the individual members.'

In reality the firm should have a new shopsign painted, reading 'Windsor and Sons and Daughter'. While each family member sells the same product their branches have separate policies and practices. Even when decisions go to the 'chairman of the board', advisors who urge caution are regularly overruled. As one former member of the Household observes, 'You can be two hundred per cent correct but if one of the Queen's children wants to do it differently you can be sure that the Queen will take their side. The first thing you learn in royal service is that her children can do no wrong.'

This fact of royal life – witness the unnecessarily messy way Prince Edward contrived his exit from the Royal Marines – is confirmed by a long-standing friend of the Queen. He said, 'The Queen has no control over her family in precisely the same way that Queen Elizabeth, the Queen Mother had no control over Princess Margaret.'

Within this creaking structure, courtiers endeavour to protect the integrity of the Crown as well as maintain the historic links between the monarchy and the ecclesiastical, military and political worlds. Naturally it falls to the press office to present the public face of the royal family, organizing photo opportunities, arranging television coverage and monitoring the mass media.

It means that everything from the choice of official historians allowed to delve into the royal archives at Windsor Castle library to the royal family's appearances on television are carefully weighed to ensure that a positive portrait of the monarchy is on show.

Control of information is the key. Unauthorized

A craftsman carefully touches up the paintwork on a landau, used to bring ambassadors to the palace.

leaks are pursued, books and memoirs by former staff are banned while sensitive historical documents are suppressed or censored. The Palace's influence is pervasive. As a former royal bodyguard noted, 'There was a constant eruption of palace investigations into leaks. We were always fearful that the finger might point at us so we tried to keep clear.' Journalists who write regularly on the royal family have their backgrounds investigated – 'We have a file on all of you guys,' the Queen's then assistant press secretary, the late Victor Chapman once revealed. While lurid talk of palace phone taps is probably a Fleet Street fantasy, courtiers prudently regulate the release of information over which they have control.

Even those writers who are unabashed monarchists find that their work is hampered if they have not been given the official seal of approval. When former *Daily Telegraph* journalist Ann Morrow embarked on a biography of the Queen her research came to a series of baffling dead ends – especially when she contacted members of the Household. A hitherto secret memo, marked 'Confidential', from the Queen's former press secretary Michael Shea to all heads of departments, indicates why. It states:

While Miss Morrow is a reputable and generally accurate and sympathetic journalist with regard to reporting of royal events and occasions, she is very persistent in her methods of research. We have already had considerable evidence that she is prepared to go to great lengths to get members of the Queen's Household, officials and staff and others who might have knowledge of a particular nature about The Queen's private life and work, to talk to her.

I would be grateful if you could draw the above note to the attention of those in your department who may in the course of their duties or privately come into contact with Miss Ann Morrow. Any members of the Household who are approached should make it clear that we are not permitted to talk to journalists about our work for The Queen. I would also be grateful if you could ask them to let me know if they have any enquiries from Miss Morrow who should, of course, be politely referred to the Press Office.

I would ask you to treat this note in the strictest confidence and no knowledge of it should of course be given to Miss Morrow herself.

With more than three miles of red carpet to maintain, keeping it clean is a full-time job.

Even members of the royal family are not immune. The Duke of Windsor was infuriated when Sir John Wheeler-Bennett, George VI's official biographer, was prevented by the Court from sending material relating to him for comment and approval. He threatened legal action before they gave way. In one letter to his solicitor Sir George Allen the Duke wrote, 'Obviously that evil snake Lascelles [the Queen's former private secretary Sir Alan Lascelles] and others have been working on Wheeler-Bennett to set my brother on a pedestal and to present me in as bad a light as possible . . . I am incensed over this latest display of rudeness towards me from the palace.'

The Duke's sentiments are instructive. Constitutionally the accepted wisdom is that the Queen can do no wrong but her ministers can, so administratively the monarch is never criticized but her courtiers are. She is the silk glove. They are the iron fist.

That friendly silk-gloved hand is formally extended every Tuesday night when the Queen meets her prime minister in a private audience. It is a ritual which symbolizes the palace's continuing position as one of the hubs of Britain's political life. The yellowing notice pinned to a wall in the footmen's room detailing the drinks required for the 40-minute meeting illustrates a sobering fact. Prime ministers, of whatever party, may come and go but the monarch treats them all in exactly the same way – right down to the gin and tonic. In fact the standing order is for gin, whisky, champagne and various tonics. Even the type of champagne flute is specified. The Queen's private secretary normally has a quiet word before the prime minister is escorted by the equerry to the pale blue Audience Chamber to give the Queen the report on the state of the nation.

Every prime minister is in agreement about the Queen's shrewd insights and remarkable eye for detail. 'The Queen was a great support because she was the one person you could talk to,' recalled the late Lord Stockton, formerly Harold Macmillan.

Winston Churchill thought she was 'lovely, she's a pet' but at the beginning of her reign she did not know him well enough to advise him to resign even though his doctor Lord Moran and other advisors wished him to go for the sake of his health. 'The late King could have done it,' they murmured.

Just as various prime ministers have leant on her wisdom, so does the Queen rely on her previous first ministers to offer their guidance on ticklish constitutional questions. Before the 1987 General Election for example, Lord Stockton sent the Queen a long letter dealing with the dangers of a hung Parliament.

The Queen's then private secretary Sir William Heseltine travelled to Lord Stockton's Perthshire home to sound out his advice. Heseltine expected a rambling lecture from a man in his dotage. Instead he was astonished to be treated to a 90-minute 'tutorial' on constitutional precedents which was 'absolutely fascinating'. He made detailed notes for the Queen's consideration.

During their relationship the Queen enjoyed Harold Macmillan's ability as a raconteur as much as his statesmanship. He once visited the Queen *en famille* only to be greeted in a state of high agitation by the late Duke of Gloucester: 'Thank Heavens you've come, Prime Minister. The Queen's in a terrible state; there's a fellow called Jones in the billiard room who wants to marry her sister and Prince Philip's in the library wanting to change the family name to Mountbatten.'

High politics is not always on the prepared agenda. The Queen showed James Callaghan around her gardens one balmy summer's evening. 'We'd talk about anything – her family, my family,' he recalls while Harold Wilson was an amusing dinner guest, all the more so because of his insistence that HP sauce take its place on the table. For once that legend was correct. Another myth, that the Queen and Mrs Thatcher enjoyed a purely businesslike relationship, has less substance. Mrs Thatcher, for all her presidential pretensions, was deeply loyal to the Crown.

Colleagues recall her instinctive reaction one evening when the rehearsal for Trooping the Colour could be heard through the windows of Downing Street. As the band broke into stirring military music she sprang to her feet, snapped crisply to attention and ordered her staff to remain silent until the end of the royal march.

The Queen exerted her right to argue with the prime minister. When Downing Street tried to stop the Queen attending the 1979 Commonwealth conference in Lusaka, Zambia to discuss the independence of Zimbabwe, the Palace sent a terse message to the prime minister. 'The Queen is head of the Commonwealth. It is in that capacity that she will go to Lusaka. She is not open to advice from the British government on this matter.'

For the palace is not only an axis of British political life; it is the constitutional focal point of the Commonwealth. As the Commonwealth is very much a creation of this reign, the Queen goes to great lengths in trying to create a sense of family among the disparate member nations. In the days when tourists could still sign the palace visitors' book, the son of a Commonwealth prime minister on a backpacking trip around Europe called in to write his name and ended up being invited to tea with the Queen the following afternoon.

There was one quintessentially English occasion when the Queen signed the document which gave her assent for Canada to fly the Maple Leaf flag – and then poured a cup of tea for the then Canadian prime minister Lester Pearson. During another visit the Queen was showing Pearson her paintings when suddenly her page appeared. He apologized for the intrusion and handed the prime minister a telegram marked 'Urgent'. Understandably Pearson did not want to accept the missive at such a time – but the Queen insisted. 'It's certain to be of great importance or it wouldn't be delivered here,' she said. The prime minister tore the envelope open. It read: 'Save our community from being turned into a parking lot' and was signed by a Toronto ratepayers' association.

Just as the red leather boxes with their gold-embossed EIIR are symbols of the Queen's domestic influence, so the daily diplomatic bags from Australia, New Zealand, Canada and other Commonwealth countries are a sign of the Sovereign's global authority. These telegrams and briefings are not always given top priority. Late one evening, just as the firm was shutting up shop, a bag from Australia arrived. 'Oh, it will wait until morning,' said a weary courtier, not realizing that the bag contained diplomatic dynamite. The next day the Palace awoke to discover that the Queen's representative Sir John Kerr had dismissed the Australian prime minister Gough Whitlam, sparking off a constitutional crisis. Secret documents relating to the affair lay unopened.

While these diplomatic bags, red boxes and prime ministerial meetings contain the script for high drama, the meeting of her Privy Council has all the ingredients for low farce. The council, which can trace its origin back to Norman times, meets in order to endorse government legislation.

The former Labour minister Tony Crosland recorded the day he received a letter of 'archaic formality' dealing with the procedure to be adopted when he was sworn in as privy counsellor. 'Five paragraphs followed on which knee to bend on successive footstools while advancing to kiss the Queen's hand and become a member of Her Majesty's Most Honourable Privy Council.'

The procedure of swearing in, which involves kneeling on stools and walking backwards without falling over, is a cause of irritation among radical politicians. Former Labour minister Richard Crossman described it as 'idiotic flummery' while footmen watch with barely suppressed mirth as weary politicians, occasionally overcome with emotion, contrive to trip over the velvet-coloured stools. 'One fell over, so we helped him up. The second time we left him on the floor,' recalls one palace footman. Footmen were on hand again to give assistance when two politicians stumbled out of a taxi into the palace's gravel courtyard before weaving their way to take part in a Privy Council.

Palace staff certainly didn't approve the day one politician, a former home secretary, brought a black plastic dustbin liner filled with dirty washing and asked a footman if he could have it washed.

While politicians may chafe, wherever the Queen goes, the Privy Council follows. Indeed the whole panoply of the Court travels with the Queen, whether it be delivering the endless rash of red boxes by helicopter to the royal yacht *Britannia* or packing away the Euthymol toothpaste and Bronnley English Fern soap from her bathroom. When she leaves Buckingham Palace tons of baggage are loaded on to army trucks by squaddies who receive twelve and a half pence and a bottle of beer for their trouble.

Then the palace lapses into silence, its beating heart stilled. While the Queen's away, jokers play. An off-duty footman once climbed into a suit of armour and waited motionless in the corridor to frighten a housemaid as she cleaned. He crept up behind her, she turned – and then swooned in a dead faint when she saw the apparition. Unfortunately he couldn't get out of the suit and had to wait until a patrolling policeman arrived.

The housemaid's terror was understandable. When the Queen is away only a skeleton staff is on duty. The wooden floors creak ominously as solitary staff hurry along, watched by the unseeing eyes of the Queen's long-dead ancestors whose portraits line the corridors.

In this silent building the imagination can play tricks. The staff who keep the pulse of the palace ticking over swear that the eerie chill in the Household Corridor betrays the presence of the ghost of Edward VII's secretary who shot himself one winter's night. They could be right. For wherever the Queen may be in the world, there is always someone, or something, guarding the family store until her safe return.

Guests who stay in the Belgian Suite are assigned palace staff to ensure that they don't get lost.

IV

BY ROYAL COMMAND

$\mathcal{P}$rince Edward's problem was exercising the minds of his eldest brother and the brightest and best inside the palace. The budding theatrical impresario was in charge of entertainment for the party of the year – Prince Charles's 40th birthday celebrations at Buckingham Palace.

His ambitious plan was to create the intimate atmosphere of a discotheque in the vaulting Picture Gallery but it soon became clear that the mating of Luther Van Dross with Sir Anthony Van Dyck was unworkable. Suddenly a courtier suggested hanging an awning to lower the ceiling.

Prince Charles was immediately interested. 'Jolly good idea,' he enthused. Then he was struck by a thought. 'I know who has a tent.' His advisors looked at him expectantly. A local scout troop perhaps? Or the director of a catering company?

'The Crown Prince of Saudi Arabia,' he continued, oblivious to the fact that the bedouin royal was 4,000 miles away in Riyadh. The Prince opened his little black book, a phone call was duly made, and his friend the Crown Prince instantly agreed to help. In traditionally relaxed Arab style, no more was heard about the offer until a couple

Princess Diana is acknowledged by guests to be the life and soul of palace parties. When she arrived for Prince Charles's 40th birthday party ABOVE, the main talking point was a splendid bedouin tent given by the Saudi Arabian royal family.

of days before the party. Finally fretting equerries were put out of their misery and told that the Saudi royal family's private jumbo jet had arrived at Heathrow's VIP terminal.

Its cargo was a fantasy out of the *Arabian Nights*. A huge silk tent, sumptuous lounge, brass tables, ornaments – and ten bedouin tribesmen who spent three days erecting this desert mirage amidst the Rubens and Gainsboroughs.

Their endeavours were the chief talking point in an evening of glamour and grandeur when Buckingham palace effortlessly reasserted its position as the only place to see and be seen.

A galaxy of European royalty and British aristocracy mixed with the stars of the entertainment world while attentive footmen and pages danced attendance. Theatrical producer Lucinda Craig Harvey, who once employed Princess Diana as a cleaner for £1 ($1.80) an hour and still jokily runs her finger across the woodwork at Kensington Palace to make sure her former employee is maintaining standards, found herself transported into a celebrity-spotters' heaven. She recalls, 'I didn't really want to sit chatting to friends. I sat open mouthed watching the celebrities and royalty parading around. It was like *Hello!* magazine come to life. Of course Diana was the life and soul, chatting to everyone, making the party go with a swing.'

Every guest was given a map which detailed the bathrooms and the position of the breakfast buffet

Rock star Phil Collins sang for his supper at Prince Charles's birthday party. He wasn't too impressed by the palace sound system which failed as he was about to start his gig.

replete with silver salvers filled with scrambled eggs and croissants. There was one hitch. When Phil Collins appeared on stage at midnight the sound system failed. 'What kind of a gig is this?' joked the balding rock singer – much to the Queen's amusement.

While Edward VII would not have approved of the music, he would have been suitably impressed by the healthy throng of royalty and aristocracy at their ease in a majestic setting. The House was back in business. Ever since the private apartments at Windsor Castle have been closed for rewiring, the palace has been used as the principal venue for stylish private entertaining.

It has proved a resounding success. Prince Charles hosted a classical concert for the Queen Mother's 90th birthday while the guest list celebrating four royal birthdays – the Queen Mother's 90th, Princess Margaret's 60th, Princess Anne's 40th and Prince Andrew's 30th – read like a who's who of leading aristocracy.

This century the modification of royal entertaining has reflected changes in society. The dreary court levees, the tedious afternoon and evening courts and the stilted presentation of debutantes have been swept away. In their place are garden parties and informal lunches which give greater social access to the Sovereign. These events have reinforced the Queen's position as the leader of society as opposed to the narrowness of Society.

High Society has gone its own way as Lady Colin Campbell observes. 'Charity balls have taken over from the palace as the fulcrum of the social season. The charity circuit is the place where the aristocracy now gather socially.' However an invitation to a private family party at Buckingham Palace remains the height of social achievement, the litmus test of those who are truly accepted.

Those social Cinderellas left out in the cold will do almost anything to bask in the glow of royal approval – as writer Neil Mackwood discovered when he visited his friend, the Argentinian polo player and socialite Luis Basualdo in New York at the time of the Wales' wedding.

Basualdo, a boon companion to the bachelor Prince, had naturally expected an invitation to the pre-wedding ball at Buckingham Palace. The stiff gold and white invitation card had failed to materialize. 'Neil, I'm going frantic because I haven't got no invitation arrive,' he complained in fractured English. 'Yet, I play polo with this man.'

Hours before the big bash he discovered that the invitation had gone to his estranged wife Lucy Pearson in London who had forgotten to forward it. Quickly he faxed a reply of acceptance. Then, in a flurry of activity, he packed a suitcase, booked a limousine to Kennedy airport and hopped on Concorde. The fact that he barely had a nickel to his name was of no concern. He had to get to the ball of the year.

However his social triumph turned to ashes. At the ball he proudly told Prince Charles that his wedding present was waiting for him at Windsor. It was a polo pony which one of Basualdo's sponsors had flown over from Argentina. When the Prince chose to ride the animal in a crucial game, he discovered that the sorry beast simply wouldn't move. In the middle of a chukka Charles dismounted and raged over to Basualdo shouting, 'Luis, what have you done? You've given me a bloody donkey.'

Basualdo's burning ambition to go to the party was well judged. Long-serving royal staff still talk about the celebrations as the high point of their days in service. As one said, 'I didn't sleep for three nights with excitement. Everyone was working so hard to prepare for all the parties.'

The wedding breakfast, held in the ballroom, revealed the palace in all its glory with gold table decorations including an Elizabeth I salt cellar, fine crystal and plate glowing beneath six white-lustre chandeliers. It was one of those rare occasions when royalty gathers *en masse*. Every crowned head of Europe was present except the Spanish royal family who were prevented from attending because of political wrangling over Gibraltar between Britain and Spain. Instead they sent three red leather suitcases as a wedding present.

For Diana, who woke up as Lady Diana Spencer and returned to the palace as a princess, the breakfast went by as a blur. She and Prince Charles and both sets of parents were in a receiving line to welcome assorted royalty and heads of state. Protocol dictates a kiss on either cheek for a royal personage of equal status and a curtsy for those of superior status. Unfortunately the Princess barely recognized many of her new royal family. One guest noted, 'You could see the confusion in her eyes. She didn't know whether to kiss, curtsy or stand on her head.' Her discomfort was not helped by Prince Andrew who insisted on reminding her that she had married his father, the Duke of Edinburgh. During the wedding ceremony the Princess had nervously switched her husband's name and had agreed to take the hand of 'Philip Charles Arthur George'.

A time of happy confusion for the bride, a day when the Queen was not only giving away a son but also opening her doors to entertain her global family. Like all the best hostesses, the Queen has an eye for the little touches. The linen napkins in the shape of the Prince of Wales's feathers, the choice of freesias – Diana's favourite flowers – for the top table for example.

This attention to detail emphasizes that this is the Queen extending hospitality in her own home. It is why butler service, rather than silver service, is the accepted form. The difference is that silver service, where a waiter serves food on to the guest's plate, is the norm in restaurants while butler service, where a page or footman offers the dish to a guest to serve themselves, is typical of a private house. As one palace footman says, 'A lot of people say "Yes, please" because they think they are in a restaurant. They look so indignant when they are asked to serve themselves.'

Those who have sampled the Queen's hospitality are pleasantly surprised by the informal and relaxed atmosphere. The footmen are quietly unobtrusive while the equerries, ladies-in-waiting and other courtiers put guests at their ease.

It is friendly but not familiar. 'Are you unwell? Are you sure you are not ill?' asked the Queen when a member of the Household had the temerity to put his elbows on the dining table. Guests do not sit in the royal presence – unless asked – nor do they lounge with their hands in their pockets as did one government minister. It is not done either to speak across the dining table: normally the Queen speaks to the person on her left during the first and second courses, turning to the guest on her right for the remainder of the meal. A silent royal reproof follows when that unwritten rule is broken. As one luncheon guest recalls, 'The Queen was sitting next to a professor and wanted to talk about drug abuse and addiction. Then someone tried to talk across. A look from the Queen was enough. She has enormous presence.'

At times her staff can assume the haughty demeanour that comes from mixing with royalty,

Prince Charles chats to Margaret Trudeau during dinner. Prince Philip taught his sons never to look down when in conversation with a lady wearing a low-cut dress, warning them that photographers could snap them in a compromising attitude.

what the Queen calls 'red carpet fever'. On one occasion a footman stood very firmly on his dignity when the Queen entertained the trade union leader Vic Feather. Throughout lunch the bluff man of the people called everyone 'comrade'. Finally the patience of one footman snapped. 'I'm not your comrade,' he hissed. Unabashed Vic replied, 'All right then, brother,' and continued his conversation with the Queen.

Royal entertaining is the delicate art of maintaining the Queen's dignity whilst ensuring the enjoyment of her guests. Not everyone is impressed. 'We had typical British gin and tonics – lukewarm and flat,' Tamara Fraser, the wife of the former Australian prime minister, commented after her visit to the palace. Indeed state and official visits are the arena where this balancing act faces its sternest test. These biannual visits show the Queen in her formal capacity as Head of State extending the hand of hospitality to another Government leader.

The full flummery of monarchy is unveiled to impress visitors when the ultimate purpose may be to seal a trade or diplomatic agreement. Here the monarchy is the public relations arm of Britain's foreign policy, the Queen and the royal family the living symbols of goodwill. The carriage procession along The Mall and the palace itself make an impressive stage for the formal embrace between nations. As former American president Ronald Reagan says, 'The state visit to Britain is the highlight of any presidential term of office.'

Occasionally that welcoming smile is extended through clenched teeth – especially when the Queen's corgis are at risk. Royal staff were mystified when an African president insisted on silver salvers piled high with raw fillet steak being delivered to the Belgian Suite, the magnificent ground-floor rooms set aside for visiting dignitaries. The riddle was solved when they discovered that he had smuggled his dogs through customs in a diplomatic 'dog kennel' to avoid Britain's strict quarantine regulations. This infuriated the Queen who feared that her darling corgis could be contaminated with rabies – or worse. They were whisked to Windsor Castle while the president was politely but coldly told that his prized pets must stay in isolation at the airport kennels.

Palace dinner parties used to be formal affairs. White tie and evening gowns were always required. While the rules are now more relaxed, guests should never forget that their hostess is the Queen.

President Ceausescu of Romania's visit in 1978 was the first by a Communist leader to Buckingham Palace – and nearly the last. The east European tyrant who was eventually executed by his own people brought his suspicious habits to the Queen's home. He offended his hostess by insisting that his own food taster checked every meal prepared by the Queen's chef to ensure that it wasn't poisoned. Footmen and pages assigned to offer 'room service' to the president and his wife were treated with extreme distrust by Ceausescu's henchmen, the dreaded Securitate. 'They thought we had guns hiding underneath our state livery,' recalls one footman. Usually these servants are a welcome sight to help visitors negotiate the maze of passages and corridors.

This function counted for little with the Communist autocrat. Even the Belgian Suite came under scrutiny. The president, assuming that his ornate Louis XVI gilt bed was bugged, marched around the palace gardens with his staff to discuss political business.

To add injury to insult, his huge entourage drank the palace dry of whisky and then purloined cases of alcohol to take back to Romania. On one occasion the then master of the Household Sir Peter Ashmore was called in as referee when a shouting match erupted between Communist

The Queen decided that only men should serve at banquets. Indeed the Sovereign oversees every detail of a formal function, from the menus to the table decorations.

It takes three days to set the table for a banquet and three days to do the washing up afterwards. Each place setting is worth around £3,000 ($5,400) although as the government pays for the meal, economies are made where possible. These days, for example, only guests at the top table are served butter while everyone else has to make do with margarine.

AN INVITATION TO THE PALACE

While banquets are formal they are not frosty affairs. Politician's wife Margaret Tebbit, who was crippled when the IRA bombed a Brighton hotel, was unable to feed herself when she was invited to a palace dinner. She turned to the Deputy Master of the Household and told him that she was going to eat her side salad with her fingers. 'You carry on Margaret,' he said – and promptly followed suit. She says, 'I have always felt that what you can do in Buckingham Palace you can certainly do elsewhere. It was one of the things that put life into perspective.'

As a considerate hostess, the Queen keeps a watchful eye on proceedings. She is aware that as soon as she has finished a course, staff remove the plates from all the guests.

The footmen, pages and butlers memorize this plan RIGHT *before serving at a royal banquet. During the meal the Palace Steward uses a system of traffic lights to avoid a pile-up of plates and other cutlery.*

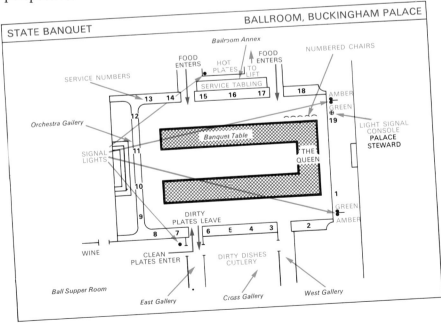

officials and weary royal staff when the thirsty guests insisted on drinking whisky at luncheon.

Whatever the Queen's personal thoughts, she duly made him a Knight of the Order of the Bath and presented him with a rifle fitted with a telescopic sight and gave his wife a gold and diamond brooch. Her diplomatic difficulties paled by contrast with those of Queen Victoria who, in 1873, allowed the Shah of Persia use of the palace. His first act was to organize a boxing match in the gardens and then, legend has it, the ruthless potentate took exception to one of his entourage and had him executed with a bowstring and buried in the gardens.

These three-day visits, which involve an army of housemaids, footmen, police and diplomatic staff, do have their lighter moments. Prince Charles was passing the Belgian Suite on his way for a morning swim during the visit of one Commonwealth leader. Suddenly he was stopped by an African valet who, thinking the heir to the throne was a footman, handed him a bundle of clothing and asked him to have it cleaned. Without a murmur, Charles accepted the dirty washing.

Normally these occasions, masterminded by the Lord Chamberlain, the senior officer of the royal Household, the Queen's Private Secretary and the Crown Equerry, work like clockwork. A glance at the timetable of former American president Jimmy Carter shows that it not only the Queen whose life is ruled by the stopwatch. 'From 10.58 to 11.14 the President talked with the First Lady' his official diary records after his return from a banquet at Buckingham Palace in 1977.

No doubt his conversation recalled with a mixture of admiration and wry amusement the moment of elaborate theatre when the Queen entered the ballroom preceded by the Lord Chamberlain and Lord High Steward walking backwards and carrying their wands of office. As Lord Cobbold, a former lord chamberlain, noted, 'All ceremony is ridiculous if it isn't perfect. The whole thing is to keep the trappings and the mystery. . . . People like it and it retains some sort of dignity. As long as it doesn't get out of balance it isn't too bad.'

The tricky manoeuvre of walking backwards is accomplished by frequent rehearsal as well as following the seams in the carpet and watching the

Sovereign. As Lord 'Chips' MacLean, the former lord chamberlain, recalled, 'She would guide me if necessary, so if I started to wobble a bit, she would gently motion with her eyes, left or right to put me back on the right track.'

This deft theatrical in an elaborate setting is meant to impress. It invariably succeeds. 'The treasures of the Nibelung!' exclaimed the wife of a German ambassador when she saw the display of gold plate and silver table decorations shimmering under the ballroom chandeliers.

It takes three days to construct this impressive stage. The fabled treasure of gold plate, silver candelabra and table decorations is carefully manhandled from the underground vault. While this priceless collection is washed and polished under the watchful eye of the Yeoman of the Gold Plate, other staff are busy pinning white linen cloths to the horseshoe-shaped banqueting table. It is the job of the table decker – usually the youngest and lightest footman – to put on a pair of slippers and walk along the table making final adjustments to the centrepieces and arrangements.

On the second day the table is laid, the position of every gold knife, fork and spoon and each one of the Brierley crystal glasses engraved with the EIIR cypher is measured by ruler. The footmen serve the meal, without the gloves they used to wear, on silver-gilt plates, the dessert on either Worcester porcelain made for William IV or eighteenth-century French Sèvres, Victorian Minton or early nineteenth-century Rockingham. Care is essential. Each place setting of silver, glass and plate is worth at least £3,000 ($5,400).

While this operation is under way, Fred Whiting who as Yeoman of the Cellars has one of the most enviable jobs in the palace, makes his preparations. He knows that the Queen, who selects the menus – usually fish, lamb or chicken – and checks the banquet herself, invariably chooses German wines. Popular myth has the cellars of Buckingham Palace as a vision of cobwebbed bottles of vintage champagne, port and fine wines. Unfortunately the reality is rather different.

Princess Diana, wearing jewellery given to her by the Queen Mother and the Saudi Arabian royal family, listens to a speech following a banquet.

In fact all wines for state lunches and banquets are supplied from the cavernous cellars at Lancaster House and organized by a civil servant, the Clerk of the Royal Cellars. The government pays for state banquets – which explains why only the top table is allowed butter. Everyone else makes do with margarine.

The royal family's cellars at Buckingham Palace are relatively small, housing private collections of vintage port laid down to commemorate royal events such as births and jubilees. Prince Philip keeps his collection of Hine cognac, vintage 1906, 1912 and 1922, while the Queen has her supply of Lanson champagne. Each bottle is chalked with the initials of the relevant royal and each time a bottle is sent to the royal apartments it is noted in a cellar book which dates back to Queen Victoria.

For a banquet, the yeoman and his staff carefully decant the claret and port and plunge dozens of bottles of white German Riesling into buckets of ice. Indeed a traditional perk for Downstairs staff

The 1844 Room was so named after a visit in the same year by Emperor Nicholas I of Russia. The Queen, who likes the small Canaletto paintings in the room, meets her guests here.

is to finish off any leftovers. In the old days servants kept used candles or 'Palace ends'. This source of income was so lucrative that it enabled William Fortnum, a footman to Queen Anne, to set up Fortnum and Mason.

As Princess Diana makes the final adjustments to her dress, an army of pages and footmen in their scarlet livery and gold braid receive their final instructions from the steward. They have already perused a 24-point guide of instructions which includes such minutiae as 'Wine Butlers also serve gravy' and 'under-butlers serve potatoes only'.

Just as guests rarely appreciate the elaborate preparations, so too they remain blissfully unaware of the fate awaiting them if they scorn the courtesies of the impassive ranks of pages and footmen. Servants call it 'striping'. A footman, burdened with heavy livery and carrying a red-hot silver-gilt 'flat' laden with food, gently touches the bare shoulder of a woman guest, invariably a British aristocrat, should she choose to ignore their requests to serve herself. Footmen can see at a glance who the worst offenders are by the multiple burn marks on their arms.

Servants, mindful of the traffic lights, know that as soon as the Queen has finished a course it is time to serve another dish. 'Everything is served together and taken away together,' says one footman. 'If you haven't finished, that's tough.' This haste does lead to hiccups. As a footman eagerly leant forward to take away the plate of a brigadier's wife, his gold braid caught up in the flimsy straps of her evening gown. He tugged away, snapping the dress strap and revealing more of her *décolletage* than she would ever have wished.

This would not have been as embarrassing at a royal banquet as elsewhere. From an early age royal princes are instructed to look into the eyes of women in evening dress. As Prince Charles once explained to actress Susan Hampshire, 'My father told me that if I ever met a lady in a dress like yours, I must look her straight in the eyes; otherwise someone might take a photograph of me in what might appear a compromising attitude.'

It is surprising that these accidents do not occur more frequently given the unfamiliar and uncomfortable costume worn by both guests and staff alike. Stiff collars and white ties are among the pet

Princess Diana complains that diamond tiaras give her a headache. However she put a brave face on her discomfort when she met President Cossiga of Italy.

hates of Prince Charles and Prince Philip. However they take punctilious pride in dressing correctly for official functions. At times guests deliberately breech House rules.

Singer Barbra Streisand loudly asked the Queen why she had to wear white gloves at a reception. 'I suppose it's the custom,' the Queen answered silkily before moving on, aware that Americans, proudly conscious of their republican heritage, create the most fuss about obeying royal protocol. When a new American ambassador to the court of George V announced that he would not wear knee breeches to the palace, then accepted etiquette, he created a minor diplomatic incident – and the King's displeasure. Even today a decision to wear black tie – rather than white tie – creates a stir. Susan Crosland, the widow of the former Labour education secretary Tony Crosland, recalls, 'Panic ensued among private secretaries until Buckingham Palace rang back to say the Queen was "very relaxed" about the education secretary's black tie.'

These stilted courtesies are exchanged for friendly informality when the Queen entertains high achievers, usually from the worlds of sport, business or the arts, to luncheon at the palace. The first such lunch was held in May 1956 when the editor of *The Times* sat down with the Bishop of London, the managing director of Wembley Stadium, the headmaster of Eton and the chairman of the National Coal Board.

For once the intricate manual of court procedure remains firmly closed as Phyllis Pearsall, the indefatigable founder of the *A–Z* guides, discovered. 'We simply lined up to meet the Queen,' she recalls. 'In fact it wasn't even as orderly as the line for Lenin's tomb in Moscow where soldiers make you smarten yourselves up. It was all rather desultory, reminding me of a column of cookhouse Wrens being taught to drill.'

Conversation is as eclectic as the variety of guests. Hindsight, creativity, left-handedness, perspective, Canaletto and George III were the subjects which absorbed guests during one stimulating luncheon last year. Even Prince Edward's love life came under scrutiny. Like many men before him, the bachelor Prince confessed his bafflement of the female sex. He told Phyllis, 'It's extraordinary. You find them really interesting and everything is going well. Then they say something and you don't like them as much any more.' Her advice was the same she gives to the lovelorn among her own staff – to see how a girlfriend behaves with those around her. 'If they are kind to others, that is a good sign,' she counselled.

While Phyllis, a sprightly 84-year-old, was relaxed about her royal encounter, others become tongue-tied or simply start babbling in the presence of majesty. The thought of dining with the Queen at Buckingham Palace can strain the nerves of even the most self-assured.

For Joy Pinder, the headmistress of Starbank School in the Midlands, the days before the lunch were the worst. She recalls, 'I felt blind panic the Sunday beforehand. When I arrived at the palace I was super hyped-up and felt every nerve in my body. I was directed up the stairs to an easel with a table plan and list of guests displayed on it. My glasses were in my handbag but I didn't trust myself to get them out. Then I saw a figure and

thought, Great, it's someone I know. It was the runner Steve Ovett who I had seen on TV. He was rather taken aback when I greeted him like a long-lost friend.'

After the master of the Household, Rear-Admiral Sir Paul Greening, told guests that it was 'very informal' the Queen walked through the door, her hand outstretched, and said, 'Mrs Pinder, thank you for coming.' Mrs Pinder recalls, 'I felt such a twit when I replied, "How do you do, Your Majesty." But that was the last time I felt subservient. The atmosphere of the place and the other people made you feel comfortable and at home. I felt that I had been to visit a friend who as genuinely interested in what I was doing.'

'I like the smaller paintings best myself,' said the Queen as she joined Phyllis Pearsall and Averill Burgess, headmistress of South Hampstead High School for Girls. She enthusiastically explained that the royal art collection had been built up because previous monarchs enjoyed the pictures rather than bowed to the dictats of contemporary fashion. 'Isn't it awful when things are done simply for fashion,' said the Sovereign. 'I have that thought every time I am on the motorway and see signs saying "Sorry for the delay". They are not sorry, simply following a fashion to be nice.'

The impression remains of a stimulating woman who is informed, interested and opinionated. Not once is the Queen's legendary passion for horse-flesh on the conversational menu. She is animated with the thriller writer P. D. James as they discuss the problems of creativity. 'I don't particularly enjoy writing but once it's over I have a sense of achievement,' she muses.

With schoolteachers she discusses the problems of the left-handed. 'My father George VI was left-handed,' the Queen says. 'I am convinced that if he

Palace staff INSET LEFT make a clean sweep before the first guests arrive for the summer garden parties which are held at Buckingham Palace and Holyrood House during July. Around 30,000 guests are invited and, while the crowds mill around the royal family INSET RIGHT, the wise wander through the 39 acres of garden which contain a rich variety of plant and animal life, including flamingos which are fed on shrimps to enhance their pink colouring.

had been allowed to write with his left hand rather than his right his stammer would not have been as bad.' Then she gives an insight into the fatalistic side of her nature. Early in life, she says, she had taught her children to accept things as they were going to be, that is to accept their royal destiny. Then she warms to her theme, arguing that there are some things – creativity, drawing and artistry – which children simply cannot be taught.

Nerves gone, the schoolmistress in Joy Pinder interrupts the monarch in mid-stream. 'You can't say that,' she says, realizing even as the words drop into the pool of conversation that majesty flows where it will. 'I can't say that. Why can't I say that?' asserts the Queen as Mrs Pinder argues, 'You can teach children perspective and draughts-manship. But you can't teach them creativity.'

That minor skirmish prepared Mrs Pinder for a major battle with Prince Philip over lunch. 'He very quickly established what kind of a headmistress I was,' she recalls. 'The Duke realized that I wasn't one of those idiot women who don't believe in competition and we had a long discussion about how people are in competition all the way through life. He was obviously a gentleman who had some firm ideas that had to be confronted. We had a heated discussion and I feel that if I hadn't challenged him he would simply have spoken to the person on his left.'

Such is the ebb and flow of discussion that guests rarely have an opportunity to appreciate the immaculate table display which is – well, fit for a Queen. For a twelve-strong luncheon party there are six palace servants on duty. Two pages are in charge of the wine, two footmen serve the meat and two under-butlers put down the plates on the polished oval table and serve the vegetables. They use distinctive serving spoons which, like the cutlery, date back to George III. Each solid-silver handle is distinguished by a crown and a lion: 'It is a sign that you are eating in the best hotel in town,' says one former royal butler.

What distinguishes the royal table setting is the absence of soup spoons and fish knives. Queen Victoria decreed that they were examples of 'modern vulgarity' and banned them from her tables.

There are five glasses to each place setting: for

white and red wine, water, port and liqueur; all are star-based Brierley crystal. The Queen has six different services for lunch, most given to her as wedding presents. The most frequently used are the green and gold Minton China plates and soup bowls which neatly complement the white and gold panelling in the lower half of the room. For dessert guests are likely to be served on a service bought by her staff to celebrate the Silver Jubilee in 1977. On each plate are hand paintings of all her horses, black Labrador gun dogs and of course her corgis. In fact her corgis sit at the Queen's feet during lunch and more than one guest has been disconcerted when the monarch has scolded, 'Eat it up' as she admonishes her dogs for leaving bits of breadstick on the carpet.

The other enduring domestic symbol of her reign, the royal handbag, is hooked underneath the Queen's place setting. It is a kind of social talisman for the monarch. Indeed the festivities for the Queen Mother's 90th birthday came to a grinding halt when the Sovereign discovered to her horror that she had mislaid that most important item in her public armoury. Footmen scurried hither and thither while guests poked about under tables until it was found in some dark corner where an aristocrat had accidentally kicked it.

The royal handbag is far more than a fashion accessory. When the Queen picks it up it is a signal that the seamless drama of monarchy is moving to another scene. At lunch it indicates to staff that they should bring the coffee and liqueurs to the adjoining drawing room. This gives the Queen the chance to speak to her other guests – and for some to reach for a cigarette. At around 2.45 p.m. the Queen leaves as she entered, a confusion of corgis at her heels. Her guests chat for a few minutes longer before they are shown out of the palace and emerge blinking into the afternoon sunlight.

'It's something to reach 84 and have the most fairy-tale and honoured day in one's life,' says Phyllis Pearsall, who framed the menu card and table plan which is always given to guests as a memento of their visit. However unauthorized souvenir hunters are the bane of royal life. Solid-silver coffee spoons engraved with EIIR are favourites although on one occasion the wife of an American ambassador was spotted slipping a silver menu-holder into her handbag. When a footman challenged her she came out with a stream of invective and walked away with her royal booty.

Garden parties at which 30,000 visitors each summer enjoy the Queen's hospitality, are the worst. When staff counted up the cutlery at the end of one garden party they discovered that nearly a thousand crested silver teaspoons had vanished. Since then uncrested stainless steel from the caterers is the order of the day.

At another garden party a clergyman secreted a collapsible butterfly net under his cassock and used it to swoop on some notable specimens for his collection. The pilfering prelate certainly picked the right garden. There are about two thousand varieties of plant and wildlife within the palace walls including a moth, hitherto unknown in Britain, which moved in following a Commonwealth Prime Ministers' Conference.

Aside from these irritating abuses of the Queen's hospitality, the garden parties – held in July at Buckingham Palace and Holyrood House – are the most striking demonstration of the royal family's continuing accessibility and popularity.

They were instituted early in the reign of Queen Victoria for the respectable classes. These 'Breakfasts', as they were then called, feature in several of Trollope's political novels. With the death of Prince Albert they were suspended and it wasn't until six years later that the widowed Queen was persuaded to resume her Breakfasts. She found them 'alarming, puzzling and bewildering' and thought visits to the zoo were less exacting. Even today the Queen Mother calls them 'zoo teas'.

Garden parties – no longer called breakfasts – were revived on a more important scale by King George V and Queen Mary. The idea was to allow the royal family to circulate without excessive formality among guests and then retire to a durbar tent for tea and further presentations.

This principle has been extended in this reign as the remaining rump of Presentation parties has been abolished and the garden party has been made the main vehicle for the Queen and her family to entertain a true cross-section of society.

So great is the preparation for all these grand tea parties that from April onwards additional staff are taken on by the Lord Chamberlain's Office to handwrite the names on the invitation cards. Guests are admitted by production of a small personal card and then efficiently ushered through the Bow Room – all white and gold, with exquisite Chelsea porcelain in glass cabinets that line the walls – before emerging into the gardens.

At four o'clock the military band, which serenades the throng with pop classics, strikes up the National Anthem as the Queen walks from the Garden Entrance accompanied by other members of the royal family. Tenants from the Duchies of Lancaster and Cornwall are first presented to the Queen who then promenades among her eager guests. The expectant multitude is efficiently marshalled by gentlemen-at-arms, armed only with rolled umbrellas, who smoothly part the way to ensure a dignified royal progress.

It was at one such garden party that Princess Diana talked about the night she and the Duchess of York dressed as policewomen to try and gate-crash Prince Andrew's stag party. She complained that the shoes were too tight and the uniform

The Duchess of York's exuberant high spirits have injected new life into the palace. The exploit when she and Princess Diana dressed as policewomen is still commented on by royal staff.

didn't fit properly. As they crane their necks for a glimpse of the Princess, women guests invariably notice that she never wears tights and even uses fake suntan on her legs.

Most guests don't even get this close such is the crowd surrounding members of the royal family as they make their way to the royal tent for tea and the reception of various Commonwealth dignitaries. Keen gardeners or regulars who know the form eschew the display of royalty to walk along the two and a half miles of gravel paths – designed so that they were wide enough for Queen Victoria's pony and trap – admiring the most splendid garden in the capital.

They envy the immaculate herbaceous borders, savour the scent from the camomile lawn and delight in the miniature temples and exotic flamingos, introduced in 1961, feeding in the lake. The birds are fed packets of shrimps to enhance their beautiful pink hues.

Today the gardens are visited by more people than at any time in their history but few realize that their expansive informality is thanks mainly to the enthusiasm of the Queen Mother. She ordered dreary Victorian shrubs and bushes to be cleared to make way for a variety of lighter foliage and decorative flowering specimens such as camellias, magnolias and cherries.

However there is one problem, a hardy annual at Buckingham Palace, that is never solved. When a garden party, or for that matter a banquet, lunch or birthday celebration, is over guests face the inevitable problem of making their way home. The euphoria of being privy to the Queen's hospitality soon gives way to despair in the futile search for a suitably dignified mode of transport. As one former mayor observes, 'You look daft done up in full morning dress on a double-decker bus.'

After Princess Anne's 40th-birthday bash, Captain Mark Phillips, who once arrived at the palace in a carriage and four, was reduced to standing in The Mall at midnight looking in vain for the beckoning bright orange light of a vacant London taxi.

Prince Charles may be able to conjure up a mirage of tents from Middle Eastern princes for his guests. But a London taxi after midnight? Now that really is magic.

V

PANIC AT THE PALACE

The black barrel of a pistol slowly peeped around the door of Princess Diana's waiting room at Kensington Palace. Her visitor smiled and continued reading his *Daily Telegraph* whilst Prince Harry crept into the downstairs chamber. 'Stick 'em up,' he cried in triumph, blissfully unaware that his mother's friend had seen him coming. A game of make-believe played by small boys the world over. The only difference between Prince Harry and millions of other seven-year-olds was that he had attached a working police radio to his 'uniform' belt for added authenticity. It had been loaned by a generous guard.

For Princes William and Harry security is a way of life. 'Are you taking my mummy away with you?' asks Prince Harry of his 'prisoner', painfully aware that the arrival of visitors to his London home often means he can no longer see his mother. Both boys know that when Princess Diana leaves she does so with a man who is friendly, fatherly, but who also carries a gun. It is not a worry. In fact

Every vehicle entering Buckingham Palace is now routinely checked by police. The mirrors are designed to show any concealed explosive devices. The Grenadier Guards ABOVE *usually perform ceremonial royal duties (here seen escorting Princess Diana as she leaves a performance of the play* Little Foxes)*, but they are also assigned to protect Buckingham Palace in times of crisis.*

it makes life rather exciting. Climbing into tanks at army barracks or riding on police motorbikes is the dream of most boys. For William and Harry it is one of the perks of a life cocooned by spy cameras and armed police.

It is their introduction to the 'bodyguard culture', the realization, which in time becomes a reflex, that someone, somewhere wants to harm you. Captain Mark Phillips gave an insight into that royal instinct when he spoke about the night an armed madman tried to kidnap Princess Anne yards from Buckingham Palace. 'I don't think it had ever occurred to me that something like that would happen. But Princess Anne had thought about it, and had got clearly in her mind what she would or wouldn't do in the circumstances.'

Again that subconscious reaction took over when Prince Andrew drove back to Buckingham Palace following his stag night. Normally the duty policeman simply waves him through. Not that night. Unbeknown to the Prince, two 'police-women', namely his bride-to-be and Princess Diana, had taken over the gate and closed it as he approached. Sensing danger, the Prince slammed his car into reverse gear, slewed round and sped off down The Mall. A copybook response to a possible terrorist attack.

His caution was entirely understandable. Buckingham Palace is the most dangerous place in the world for the Sovereign and her family. During the 150 years the royal family has lived at the Palace its members have suffered assassination attempts, shootings, kidnaps, break-ins and burglaries. Queen Victoria survived at least seven attempts on her life and on one occasion in 1842 she acted as an assassin's decoy.

Throughout her reign the Queen put her trust in God and the bravery of her servants rather than the strong arm of the law. Her instincts proved true. Her cries of 'Save me' brought her loyal retainer John Brown racing to the rescue when, in February 1872, a republican Irishman tried to kidnap her at pistol point just outside the Garden Entrance to the palace.

Indeed, in spite of the ever present threat from the Irish Republican Army or the lone madman, Queen Victoria's unswerving belief in the Almighty as the principal source of protection has permeated through to the present reign. That conviction was also shared by the Queen's subjects. In 1952 when just one personal protection officer was on duty at Trooping the Colour it was no coincidence that four out of ten of the British people believed that the Queen was chosen by God.

A generation later, in 1981, there were 3,500 police on duty but that didn't prevent Marcus Sarjeant firing six shots, all blanks, at the Queen. The only casualty was the insignia of the Order of the Garter which jolted from her tunic as the monarch tried to control the usually biddable Burmese. Fortune smiled again. It was recovered and returned before the Queen acknowledged the cheers of relief and admiration from the balcony.

That relaxed, almost fatalistic, view of royal protection meant that at Buckingham Palace the security provided by Scotland Yard was seen as a rather unnecessary intrusion. Bodyguards were trained to melt into the background. 'It was the biggest compliment to an officer if he were mistaken for the Queen's private secretary,' Commander Michael Trestrail, the Queen's former bodyguard, would tell new recruits as they busily bought themselves the waterproof green Barbours, brown trilbys and wellington boots that are the off-duty uniform of the Household.

Trestrail fitted in because he busied himself with those tasks which gave him proximity to the Queen without drawing attention to himself. He carried her umbrella and supplies of Malvern water and attentively placed a blanket around the Queen's knees when she was seated in her limousine. Trestrail, who jokingly referred to himself as 'Aquarius, the water carrier', performed these duties for a sensible purpose. As he pointed out to recruits, these chores put the bodyguard between the Queen and a potential problem at a critical moment without appearing too obvious.

It was a major triumph when the Sovereign agreed to be accompanied by motorbike outriders for an engagement. They may be commonplace today but the language of security harks back to cosier days. When a detective drives out of Buckingham Palace with a member of the royal family they still call it travelling 'on the box', a reference to the front seat of a Victorian coach.

The attempt by Ian Ball in 1974 to kidnap Princess Anne from her limousine as she was travelling along The Mall to Buckingham Palace forced a major revision of close protection. While personal protection was reformed, the business of guarding the palace was largely ignored.

During the 1970s, as the IRA mounted its big-

The Queen with her former bodyguard Commander Michael Trestrail (right), who believed that a close protection officer should melt into the background.

gest mainland bombing campaign since the Second World War, palace security was casual bordering on the complacent. When nannies took their royal charges for walks in the royal parks they were armed with a whistle, kept under a pram blanket, to blow in case of attack. As one former royal nanny recalls, 'All it did was make you very nervous about taking the children for a walk. You saw everyone as a potential kidnapper.'

Security was so lax that when Prince Charles, then a Cambridge student, celebrated his 21st birthday, an undergraduate from the rival Oxford University was able to gatecrash the party by climbing over the garden wall. The drunken student was eventually ejected but not before he had insulted the Queen. 'I saw him,' she recalled, 'and he was so drunk that he couldn't say anything apart from a few incivilities.'

Many of the uniformed police attached to the palace were either men close to retirement or youngsters who wanted time to study for promotion exams. 'Officers had been found paddling in the goldfish ponds and one man was in bed with a maid when he should have been on duty outside the Queen's bedchamber,' former officer Brian Hilliard claimed.

The resistance to change came from the top. When Sir David McNee, then the commissioner of the Metropolitan Police, attempted to implement recommendations to improve palace security, he faced procrastination from all the Queen's men.

One man, Michael Fagan, did what the IRA, the Metropolitan Police, the Home Office and the Department of the Environment could not. He changed the guard at Buckingham Palace. It is now a bristling fortress with its own police station – suitably screened by trees so that the Queen doesn't see it when she is walking the corgis – bullet-proof police boxes, and Israeli-developed technology including infra-red beams, trembler devices and spy cameras.

The days when staff threw suspect packages against a wall to see if they exploded are gone. Instead a sensitive fluorscope monitors all the mail while the legendary SAS are said to have tested the defences at least five times, on one occasion taking away a silver trophy as a souvenir.

In the past the only occasion when the 39 sen-

Marcus Sarjeant is arrested after firing six blank shots at the Queen during the 1981 Trooping the Colour ceremony. As the Queen tried to control her startled horse Burmese, the insignia of Order of the Garter tumbled from her tunic.

tries and four officers on guard outside the palace were armed was on the night of Edward VIII's abdication. Not any more. While live ammunition has always been kept in the guard room, soldiers on duty now carry six bullets in a plastic pouch as a matter of routine. At times of heightened tension the guards are armed. So when the IRA attempted to assassinate the prime minister with a rocket attack on Downing Street in 1991, the palace went on to 'amber alert'. All entrances and all internal doors were shut tight and the Officer of the Guard gave the command, 'Load your weapon.'

Even the Royal Standard, which flutters above the palace when the Queen is in residence, has succumbed to the security assault. On several occasions when the Queen has privately visited Wood Farm on her Sandringham estate, the flag, which should be lowered immediately the Queen leaves, has remained aloft as a decoy. That did not fool Michael Fagan.

While it was Fagan's second visit, when he

entered the Queen's bedroom, which created the international furore, it was his first entry in the summer of 1982 that was potentially the most dangerous. Just five hours after President and Nancy Reagan had landed at Heathrow airport, Michael Fagan was scaling a drainpipe inside the grounds of Buckingham Palace – a key venue during the state visit.

That evening, as the President and the Queen Mother blithely recited all eleven verses of the Robert Service poem 'The Shooting of Dan McGrew' over dinner at Windsor Castle, Scotland Yard chiefs made a critical judgment. They decided to keep secret from the American Secret Service the fact that Buckingham Palace had been entered by an unknown intruder.

If they had been warned it could have put the entire presidential visit in jeopardy. They were acutely aware that the American Secret Service are notoriously cautious about presidential safety and, ever since the Blunt, Burgess, Maclean and Philby spy scandals, have had scant regard for British intelligence or security. Indeed on one occasion when President Gerald Ford was dining on board the royal yacht *Britannia*, the Secret Service insisted that an armed guard sit behind him – much to the Queen's annoyance.

President Reagan with the Queen, oblivious of the fact that before he arrived at the palace police had searched in vain for an intruder who startled a housemaid. It was in fact Michael Fagan.

At the time of the break-in no one knew for certain if they were facing a *Day of the Jackal* scenario with a lone assassin hidden in the palace roof, his sniper's sights waiting to focus on the leader of the Western world. The president's schedule included a helicopter flight from Windsor Castle to the lawns of Buckingham Palace where he would drive along The Mall to meet Prime Minister Margaret Thatcher at Downing Street.

That security nightmare began at twenty minutes past eleven on the evening of 7 June 1982. It was a warm night and housemaid Sarah Carter was lying on her bed reading a book. Suddenly she noticed a hand appear outside her open bedroom window. She screamed and ran out into the corridor where she saw two friends, who were also housemaids. While they went to alert the duty policeman Sergeant Geoffrey Braithwaite, Fagan, dressed in jeans and a teeshirt, clambered into the room, leaving a trail of sticky pigeon repellent on the carpet.

Fagan recalls, 'The drainpipe was at least fifty-five feet and I climbed it in seconds. I felt I could do anything, touch the sky, anything. I was a Prince of the Earth. I climbed in and idled my time walking up and down the passageway. I was at my leisure, looking at the paintings and wandering about the corridors.'

As Fagan continued his tour, Sergeant Braithwaite had visited the bedroom, organized a search and then phoned other police divisions for reinforcements. Among them was Rochester Row where Detective Sergeant Rodney Whicheloe was on duty. He was told to call his superior officer and bring him to the palace.

As the Yard's finest were roused from their beds, Fagan was in the room once used by Prince Charles's nanny Mabel Anderson. When Fagan entered, in search of a glass of water, room 108 was used to store presents for Princess Diana's expected first child. Instead of water he slaked his thirst with a bottle of Californian Riesling which he found on top of a cupboard. Then he waited for his 'host', the Duke of Edinburgh.

He recalls, 'I had it all worked out. I was waiting for Prince Philip to come. After all it's his house. I wanted him to come in and say, "What are you doing here?" then I would have replied, "I've come to see the Queen." Anyway I waited and waited and as no one came I got rather bored. I opened the door and saw a policeman with a dog. When he went I nipped down the stairs, climbed through a window and went home.'

As Fagan's adventure ended, Whicheloe's was just starting. He and his superior officer, a detective chief inspector, began by interviewing the maid, Sarah Carter. They soon had doubts about the hand at the window when she admitted that she had been to a seance that night.

However the finger marks on the windowsill and the pigeon repellent lent credence to her story. The search continued as another Scotland Yard chief arrived to take command. 'Looks like we have an intruder, sir,' Whicheloe and his colleague reported. 'Christ,' came the reply, 'Reagan arrives today. Has anyone notified the American Secret Service that we have a problem?'

When the Scotland Yard officer realized that word had not yet reached American ears he ordered that they should be kept in the dark. In the mean time the search continued. As dawn was breaking, Whicheloe was deputed to drive the senior officer to Cannon Row police station. During the short journey, his boss uttered words which were to haunt him. 'My God, what a cock-up. Think of the scandal if this ever gets out.'

A caveat must be entered about Whicheloe. The former detective recounted his tale to crime writer Jeff Edwards before he embarked on his own career of blackmail and extortion for which he is now serving a long jail sentence. However, whatever the doubts about Whicheloe's testimony, it is a matter of record that Reagan visited Buckingham Palace, that Fagan entered the building and that a search was undertaken.

It is extremely doubtful, given the history of the American Secret Service, that they would have allowed their President to land on the lawns at Buckingham Palace if they had known about the intruder. Prudence would have dictated a change of plan. Certainly the evidence points to a cover-up by the authorities so that Reagan's visit could proceed on schedule. There is a final irony. As Reagan drove along The Mall to Downing Street he waved to Michael Fagan who was then still another face in the crowd.

His anonymity was not to last much longer. Fagan was reaching his wits' end. A builder's labourer, he had been out of work for months. Debts were mounting, his wife Christine was being unfaithful and he felt that his four children were suffering. The voices in his head grew louder as he teetered on the brink of a nervous breakdown. He had visions, climbed every bridge over the River Thames to test himself and swam naked in Regent's Park lake and the Grand Union Canal.

The palace had been a challenge. It had been easy. Now the voice told him to see the Queen. It was a quest he accepted. In his eyes it all seemed so simple. Climb over the wall, walk along the corridor and into the Queen's bedroom. Nothing to it. The Queen would understand, the Queen would help him bring back Christine and the children.

These thoughts, these voices were whirling round his head on the evening of 8 July. He couldn't sleep and he was happy to accept the offer of a drink from his new neighbour, mini-cab driver John Rivers who had just finished work. It was three in the morning. They made desultory conver-

Princess Anne's bullet-riddled limousine is examined by police following a bloody kidnap attempt in The Mall in 1974. The white Ford Escort was used by the unsuccessful abductor, Ian Ball. Scotland Yard revised security following the incident.

sation over a couple of glasses of whisky before Fagan left to wander the streets of Highbury in north London where he lived.

As he walked through Berwick Street market in Soho he spotted a magazine with the Queen's face on it. The Queen looked so much older than the image he had in mind. No matter. He decided then and there to speak to her about the voices in his head and the turmoil in his heart.

The palace railings presented no obstacle. He had no fear of the guards and found an unopened ground-floor window which took him into the Stamp Room which houses one of the finest stamp collections in the world. That interior door was locked so he went outside again and scrambled up a drainpipe to the flat roof above the Ambassadors' Entrance. He took off his sandals and socks to tightrope across thin bird netting which he knew would not take his weight. But the voices were driving him on. Before he attempted this feat, he spotted an unlocked window which led to the office of Vice-Admiral Sir Peter Ashmore, then master of the Household.

He recalls, 'I'd been through every kind of fear you could imagine and I just wanted to see the Queen by this time. It was a burning ambition. It had taken weeks to build up to this. Now I wanted to see her. I was going to smash a window to get in but I realized it was open.

'Then all at once I'm in the palace and I'm walking along. The carpet was soft on my feet and the floorboards were squeaking. I was surprised to see a maid vacuuming. Somehow you don't expect ordinary people in a palace. I just gave her a wave, said "Good morning" and walked on. Then I spotted a picture called *Pythagoras' Theorem* which I rather liked. I sat down and looked at it for about five minutes. I was in no hurry.

'It was getting quite light by this time and I found myself in the Throne Room. We all have delusions of grandeur and we all like to play silly games. First I wiped my hands on the curtains before I sat down because they were covered in black tar from the drainpipe. The curtains fell to bits in my hands. I tried each throne for size, rather like Goldilocks and the Three Bears. But I was not impressed. In fact the palace didn't live up to my dreams of what a palace should be.'

The liveried footmen behind the Queen Mother and Princess Diana in the Ascot procession are not all they seem. One is an armed bodyguard, an innovation advocated by Prince Charles.

As luck would have it, he accidently pressed a hidden handle in the dado rail which opens a secret door leading to the Queen's private apartments. He relieved himself in the bowls of dog food outside the corgis' room and then found his way from the King's Corridor and thence into the Queen's rooms. Moments later his odyssey would culminate with that idealized meeting with the Queen.

Up to this point his tale tallies with the official report into the incident compiled by Assistant Metropolitan Police Commissioner John Dellow. From here, until his arrest, their paths diverge. The Dellow report and other accounts describe how the Queen was wakened to discover in her bedroom not her female dresser but a barefooted Fagan, in jeans and teeshirt emblazoned 'Lonsdale', clutching a broken glass ashtray with which he intended to slash his wrists. She pressed the alarm bell and then made the first of two calls to the palace telephonist to send police to her bedroom.

As the Queen waited for the police, she reacted in textbook police style by remaining calm and collected. She listened to Fagan's tale of woe about his wife, his money troubles and his concern about poor palace security. In turn she chatted about her own children, pointing out that Prince Charles was about Fagan's age.

Six minutes later the Queen made a second call, coolly asking why there had been no response. Then she used the pretext of Fagan's craving for cigarettes to summon a maid, Elizabeth Andrew, to her bedroom. When she saw Fagan sitting on the edge of the Sovereign's bed the startled housemaid uttered the immortal phrase: 'Bloody hell, Ma'am. What's he doing in here?'

Together they managed to usher him into a pantry where they were subsequently joined by footman Paul Whybrew who had just returned from walking the corgis. The Dellow report states: 'While Her Majesty kept the dogs away as the man was getting agitated, the footman helped to keep Fagan in the pantry by supplying him with cigarettes until first one and then another police officer arrived to remove him.'

The gospel according to Michael Fagan is very different and, perhaps surprisingly, less melodramatic. This is the scene as he remembers it. 'Suddenly I open this door and there's a little bundle in the bed. I thought, This isn't the Queen, this is too small. I looked at the bed from one side and then the other but I can't believe that this is the Queen. If it was Princess Diana I was going to go because it's the Queen I've come to see. So rather than

The lone assassin in the crowd is the constant nightmare for a bodyguard. When an enthusiastic well-wisher lunged at Princess Diana during a walkabout, her detectives quickly went into action.

make a mistake I went to the curtains and lifted them. A shaft of light shone through so I must have disturbed her.

'All of a sudden she sat up and looked at me. She must have been in a deep sleep because she looked really disturbed. Her face was a mask of complete shock and incomprehension. "What are you doing here, get out, get out," she said. Her cut-glass accent really startled me. I just looked at her and replied, "I think you are a really nice woman." I said it with sincerity.

'She just repeated, "Get out, get out," and picked up a white telephone which was by her right-hand side. She didn't have to dial or anything. She said a few words in it and then she just hopped out the bed, ran across the room and went out of the door. I say "hopped" because I was quite surprised at how nimble she was. She hopped out and ran across the room like a girl. That was when I spotted her height, that she was only small.

'It was all over within thirty seconds. I knelt on the bed as she ran out. I sat down thinking, Oh hell, what have I done? I was exhausted anyway. I had been up all night and had made it here. I had tears running down my face. I felt really sad and disillusioned, it was a complete shock because the Queen wasn't what I expected.

'I felt so badly let down. She didn't live up to my vision. It was the realization that there was no one left to understand me. I just felt this incredible sadness. There were tears rolling down my face. If there had been a mirror in the room it would have shattered because at that moment all my illusions, all my dreams had been smashed to pieces.

'Everyone goes on about this conversation that we had. It simply never took place. I could elaborate and make up something which happened during those six minutes. This is the truth and it is very straightforward. Remember we are talking about a stranger waking a woman up first thing in the morning. The last thing she was going to do was to humour me.'

He denies he ever saw a chambermaid and certainly Elizabeth Andrew's parents would agree. 'What has been said about her is total myth,' said her mother.

In the semi-darkness Fagan sat slumped on the Queen's bed, blood oozing from his right thumb he had cut with a broken ashtray. He says he intended to use the glass to cut the pigeon netting as he made his escape – not to slash his wrists. His next recollection was seeing the figure of footman Paul Whybrew framed in the bedroom doorway. He took him into the Page's Vestibule, poured him a Famous Grouse whisky and brushed aside his pleas to see the Queen. 'Later, later, later,' he said, although Fagan realized there would be no further opportunity to see the Queen.

It was only then that Fagan says that he asked for a cigarette. Fagan recalls, 'I wasn't going to ask the Queen for a cigarette because I never had the chance.' Whybrew, now the Queen's assistant page, has since told colleagues that when he returned from walking the corgis he was summoned to the Queen's dressing room. He immedi-

The comfortable Regency Room, located in the north-west corner of the palace, is used as a private sitting room. Although the Queen is described as the world's richest woman, she prefers cosy rather than opulent surroundings.

ately realized something was wrong because of the unwritten rule that a male member of staff is not allowed into a royal bedroom suite.

The Queen, by now in a dressing gown, said to him, 'Can you give this man a drink?' Whybrew, astonished by the Queen's calm demeanour, took an unprotesting Fagan into the Page's Vestibule. As he poured him a whisky, Whybrew heard the Queen screaming down the telephone in her study demanding to know why the police hadn't arrived. 'I have never heard the Queen so angry,' he has told colleagues.

This second, albeit unofficial, scenario does seem plausible. Fagan repeatedly asked to see the Queen when PC Bob Roberts and his colleague finally arrived on the scene. As Fagan points out, 'I told them I wanted to speak to the Queen because she hadn't given me a chance to say anything. If I had spoken to her for ten minutes I wouldn't have had much else to say to her, now would I?'

Before he was arrested Fagan told them his name was Michael Hess and that his father was Rudolf Hess who lived in Spandau prison. Fagan says, 'They looked at me and they could see their careers just seeping through the carpet. I felt sorry for the old boys because the palace was just a retirement post.' Fagan was taken to Cannon Row police station where he was fingerprinted, footprinted and questioned as a prelude to his appearance in Number One court at the Old Bailey and life of international notoriety.

The subsequent inquiry revealed a whole catalogue of blunders, both bizarre and comic, which had allowed Fagan to reach the Queen's bedside. Alarm beams had not worked or had been switched off, the officer summoned to the Queen's assistance paused to change into his smartest uniform and an earlier superficial search of the palace, sparked by an off-duty policeman who had seen Fagan behaving suspiciously, revealed nothing. As luck would have it Fagan had chosen the moment when the internal palace doors had just been unlocked for the cleaners, when the Queen's footman was walking the dogs and when the police officer who sits outside the Queen's bedroom had gone off duty. Odds of millions to one.

The Queen was as annoyed that her domestic affairs had become a matter of consuming public interest as she was that the imperfect roulette wheel of security had allowed Fagan to hit the jackpot. 'Give her a cuddle, Philip,' said the *Daily Mirror* as the nation discussed the separate sleeping arrangements of the Sovereign and her consort. In fact the Duke had stayed the night at White's Club where he has rooms before leaving early in the morning to exercise his horses.

There were further unhappy consequences. Michael Rauch, a male prostitute, read about the Fagan incident and visited the offices of the *Sun* newspaper to tell them about his own affair with the Queen's bodyguard, Commander Michael Trestrail. The newspaper contacted Scotland Yard. Trestrail was questioned, confirmed the truth of the allegations and promptly resigned. The then home secretary William Whitelaw, who implemented the Bridge Commission to investigate security aspects of Trestrail's case, describes the shocking series of events as 'too bizarre'.

There were those inside the palace who rather wished the entire affair had been tidily swept under the red carpet. 'It was in the interest of the Home Office and Buckingham Palace officials that the whole story was not told,' Sir David McNee, the former Metropolitan Police commissioner observed in his memoirs. As one senior palace courtier told writer Douglas Keay, 'I think when such an incident does happen, there is no immediate urge in an organization like ours to rush to the public prints with it because in many ways it can be best and most reasonably investigated and any fault in the system put right in private rather than in public.'

Certainly this 'Nanny knows best' attitude which characterizes the higher echelons of the British Civil Service has worked effectively in the past. The discreet way palace officials and the police handled a hitherto unpublicized theft from the seemingly impregnable vaults deep beneath Buckingham Palace is a classic example. Banner headlines like 'Burglary at the Palace' were neatly avoided whilst the culprit was suitably chastised. It was an 'inside job' and the matter was dealt with internally. Justice was done, if not seen to be done.

Until a former air-raid shelter was transformed into a secure vault, many of the palace's valuables were held behind a locked iron cage – easy pick-

Liveried footmen and butlers are on hand when the spacious Carnarvon Room is used as a dining room. Menus are in French, the cutlery dates back to George III and the glassware is Brierley crystal.

ings for a crack burglar. The underground vault, containing silver and gold plate, heirloom jewellery, gifts, and Fabergé, can only be reached with difficulty. Every visitor, usually footmen or under-butlers from the Silver Pantry collecting table decorations for a dinner, must be accompanied by the Yeoman of the Gold Plate. He holds the keys to the grilles which open the door of the hydraulic lift which goes down to the vault. Only the Yeoman knows the combination for the fourteen-inch-thick metal door which guards the entrance to the vault.

Once inside, where a cornucopia of wealth is revealed, security is the watchword. Each member of the royal family has their own locked vault for the storage of expensive gifts, usually acquired from overseas tours. Everything is labelled, photographed – a sensible practice started by Queen Victoria – and described in a detailed inventory which runs to numerous leather-bound volumes.

Imagine then the surprise of uniformed officers who found an Aladdin's cave of eclectic royal memorabilia when they entered the London apartment of a former palace servant. The visit, which took place shortly after the Queen's Silver Jubilee, was the result of an unconnected incident. As they looked round the room they saw a Royal Standard being used as a bedspread, cotton sheets from Windsor Castle, a set of peer's robes, solid-silver cutlery bearing George III's cypher, an illuminated royal Bible and Queen Mary's engagement ring. While the haul was hardly on the scale of the Great Train Robbery, it would certainly have been embarrassing if it had become public.

The culprit, who confirmed salient features of this extraordinary episode to the author on a confidential basis, claims that he was questioned for three days by the Metropolitan Police. After due liaison with the royal Household, it was agreed that, as the stolen goods were for personal use rather than resale, no further action would be taken. The thief has a more sensational explanation for the case being dropped, claiming that he threatened to reveal extensive details about prostitution at the palace. Shortly afterwards a footman was summarily dismissed.

If all these outlandish incidents prove anything, they demonstrate that behind the impassive façade, Buckingham Palace is far more than just another government office block. It acts as a magnet for the outsider, the lonely and the plain curious, a beacon of the bizarre. Just as the royal family's schooling teaches them equanimity and caution, so they view many of the weird episodes of palace life with a stoical shrug of the shoulders. They have learned to trust very few palace staff which is why when their confidence is betrayed, the hurt is all the more painful.

Princess Anne suffered that anguish when, on 5 April 1989, she discovered that letters written to her by the Queen's then equerry Commander Timothy Laurence had been stolen from her briefcases. The culprit could only have been a person who knew of their secret relationship, had access to her personal files and, as they never asked for money, wanted revenge on either the Princess or the dashing equerry.

When Scotland Yard's fingerprint officer set up shop in the Centre Room, the chamber which leads to the first-floor balcony, it seemed to symbolize the awful indignity surrounding this episode. In the same room where the royal family gathers

Princess Anne at Ascot accompanied by Commander Timothy Laurence and the Queen's racing manager Earl Carnarvon. Laurence's letters to the Princess sparked a Scotland Yard inquiry.

prior to parading before its adoring public, a series of palace staff waited to be fingerprinted and questioned in a criminal investigation. Princess Anne, Commander Laurence and Captain Mark Phillips went through the process where their hands were laid on an ink pad and their fingers rolled across a pre-printed sheet.

The first act in this drama unfolded when John Kay, a *Sun* reporter, contacted the offices of the Royal and Diplomatic Protection Group – formed after the Fagan affair – and told them that his paper had 'sensitive and intimate' letters which they wanted to return to Princess Anne.

Commander John Cracknell, head of the Royal Protection Group, went to the newspaper's Wapping headquarters to collect the four letters. On his return he phoned the Queen's then private secretary Sir William Heseltine who later spoke to the Metropolitan Police Commissioner Sir Peter Imbert. That night the letters were back at the palace when an angry and distressed Princess Anne verified that indeed they did belong to her. The Princess, furious at this gross intrusion into her private life, told Sir William that she wanted the full weight of the law to come down on the thief.

That emphatic message was relayed to Sir Peter Imbert who called in Commander Roland Penrose, the head of his elite Serious Crime Squad, and told him to put his best man on the case. His choice was Detective Superintendent Roy Ramm, a bright cockney with an excellent track record investigating blackmail and extortion cases.

Superintendent Ramm recalls, 'I was struck by Princess Anne's forthrightness, her candour and her knowledge of ordinary people and the ways of the world. The theft had left her with a very real feeling of hurt and betrayal. The knowledge that someone close was prepared to stoop so low had cut deep. She left us in no doubt that she wanted the culprit found and punished.'

During their 80-minute conversation they soon realized that a palace employee must be the offender. The Princess acknowledged that her friendship with Commander Laurence was an open secret and went on to explain that the letters had been in several of the six briefcases which travelled everywhere with her in the locked boot of her Reliant Scimitar or official limousine.

Her cases were in a chaotic state, stuffed with everything from charity briefing papers, details of royal engagements, diaries, keys, make-up and lipstick. Her love letters were simply part of that jumble. Therefore the thief had to be someone who not only knew about the relationship but also had the opportunity to rifle through the cases.

Revenge, malice and jealousy were the motives under discussion when the two officers returned to the Yard following their preliminary investigation. As they prepared to continue, they were told that the Queen had personally intervened in the case. She had overruled her daughter and decided that under no circumstances should the thief be prosecuted. However the Palace still wanted the miscreant apprehended. It meant that the detectives were effectively acting as private investigators.

By now around seventy palace staff, ranging from housemaids to Anne's private secretary, were asked to come to the balcony room for fingerprinting and to be interviewed by the five-strong team of detectives.

Commander Laurence, the man at the centre of the storm, was interviewed for over an hour at his London flat. He was beside himself with anger and remorse but enough of a student of history to see the parallels between himself and George VI's equerry Group Captain Peter Townsend who fell in love with Princess Margaret. They even shared the same room, number 142, just along the corridor from Princess Anne's apartment.

The 36-year-old Navy officer had already checked to see if letters from Princess Anne to him had been taken and he was relieved to discover that they were still in his files. He felt sorry that Princess Anne had been dragged into this business even though he pointed out that the publicity was more damaging for him than her. While it was his assessment that it was a malicious theft with the intention of embarrassing the couple, he could not name anyone who bore him a grudge.

An unsatisfactory outcome to an affair which left only victims in its wake. Just as the Fagan incident abruptly ended an era where palace security was a civilized stumble from one compromise to another, so the theft of Princess Anne's letters has cast a long shadow across the atmosphere of cordiality and mutual trust that was once taken for granted in the royal village. The last decade has seen the flak jacket, the armed soldier and the spy camera become a fact of palace life. These days the Queen sleeps more easily in her bed but the Palace has paid a high price for that peace of mind.

Princess Anne visits the palace post office which annually handles around 75,000 items of mail. Her controversial letters from Commander Laurence were delivered to her first floor rooms in the palace by hand.

VI

POMP ON PARADE

*J*ewellery and horses are as much a part of the lexicon of kings and queens as thrones and palaces. The diamond-encrusted crown and the prince in shining armour at the head of his troops are enduring emblems of monarchy. Gorgeous jewels handed down from generation to generation reinforce the sense of family continuity while the sight of royalty on horseback is resonant with images of control, authority and superiority.

If, as George VI once argued, a sword is a sign of an officer, then a horse is the mark of a monarch. Playing polo or riding to hounds seems a proper recreation for the heir to the throne. This philosophy is accepted by Princess Diana who, while disliking these mettlesome quadrupeds, is conscious of the need to school her sons in this fundamental princely art.

The clatter of hooves across the courtyard at Buckingham Palace and the sight of the Queen and the Princess of Wales in an immaculate coach in all their jewelled finery symbolize the splendour and pageantry that is the public face of the modern monarchy. Indeed the Trooping the Colour ceremony seems rather like an elaborately iced cake without a cherry on top since the Queen decided to

Buckingham Palace is the grand setting at times of public or royal celebration. The 50th anniversary of the Battle of Britain was a perfect example of the way monarchy continues to represent national life.

lead the parade in civilian dress seated in a state landau rather than riding side-saddle in the scarlet tunic and tricorn of her Household regiments.

The intimate and enduring relationship between the horse and royalty is revealed by a glance at the imposing Royal Mews adjacent to Buckingham Palace. These luxuriously appointed stables, designed by Nash in 1825, are an important part of the palace establishment. While the Crown Equerry, who has under his control 11 chauffeurs and 39 grooms and coachmen, runs the fleet of royal limousines, it is the Cleveland Bays and Windsor Greys who receive most of his attention. For it is these well-bred, even-tempered carriage horses who are the real Rolls-Royces of royal pomp and circumstance. It is a wise choice. While kings are on record as swapping their kingdoms for a horse, there are no examples of similar transactions for an automobile.

The Prince of Wales would not have it any other way. As he says, 'I would change nothing. Besides ceremony being a major and important aspect of monarchy, something that has grown and developed over a thousand years in Britain, I happen to enjoy it enormously.'

At occasions like Trooping the Colour or the State Opening of Parliament, the crowds marvel at the undulating landscape of scarlet, gold and silver, the precision and the pageantry. The Windsors watch for the particular: the misplaced decoration, the sloppily executed manoeuvre that only the trained eye could spot. A BBC producer discovered this Windsor characteristic when the Queen's private secretary enquired why a dance troupe had been clearly shown clicking their gloved fingers on television whilst the sound was of fingers uncovered. The Queen's sharp eye and ear had spotted the difference. It resulted in a memo to her private secretary and an explanation of post-sound synchronization.

This unerring eye for detail is a family tradition, nay obsession, and royal traditions die hard. An explanation by George VI's courtiers could equally well apply to the Queen and Prince Charles. 'It is a different type of mind from ours . . . the king, for instance, minds criticism for things that do not matter and simply ignores it when applied to things that do. For instance he minds any suggestion of incorrect dress or deportment but does not care at all if it is suggested that he looks bored or cross or has no intellectual tastes.'

The Queen sends pointed memos to Household officers letting them know that a parade was below par, royal dukes take competitive pleasure in the niceties of military uniform and woe betide the valet who puts out the wrong piece of ceremonial

The Queen admires her dependable horse Burmese with Princess Margaret.

kit. Even Fleet Street's finest have felt this royal displeasure. At the end of a service at St Paul's Cathedral, the Duke of York spotted two reporters in seats allocated to the RAF. 'Why were you there?' he asked with quizzical irritation. 'It's because we're high-fliers, sir,' was the nonchalant reply.

However, even princes manage to maintain a sense of proportion in the face of the arcane absurdity of some ceremonial. On one occasion the Duke of Edinburgh was involved in an earnest discussion about whether, during the State Opening of Parliament, the over-heavy Sword of State should be held in an at-ease position rather than held aloft when the Queen made her speech.

He commented drily, 'Incidentally the "Sword" walks beside the "Cap of Maintenance", which is carried on a stick. I'm not sure what could be done with that standing at ease. Come to think of it, only the English would think of carrying a hat on a stick at a ceremony of state.'

These obscure considerations are all part of the gorgeous theatre of royal spectacle. However when the Duke of Kent's daughter Lady Helen Windsor carried her gin and tonic on to the palace balcony during the flypast at Trooping the Colour, it seemed that she was treating the occasion like an interval at a West End show. After all, there is theatre and there is theatre – and the Palace puts on a better show than anyone else in town.

It takes remorseless planning, attention to detail and endless practice to mount a handsome display like Trooping the Colour. More than 200 horses and 2,000 men spend weeks rehearsing the complex manoeuvres. On the day of the ceremony many are up before dawn polishing their boots and buttons, brushing their bearskins and grooming their faithful steeds.

The Queen, who has performed in every Trooping since 1951, is the only woman taking part. In the days when the Queen rode side-saddle, she and her horse Burmese would walk round the palace gardens, the royal corgis yapping at her fetlocks and staff banging pots and waving miniature Union Jacks to prepare the black mare for the noise of the crowds. 'If Burmese can survive that attack, then the horse will be able to survive anything,' noted the monarch.

Burmese was a present from the Royal Canadian Mounted Police and had been the Queen's mount at Trooping for eighteen years until she was retired in 1986. While the official reason was because the huge horse was too old the decision came as a welcome relief for the Queen. She told the late Lord Vaizey that riding side-saddle for two hours was such a painful test of endurance that she needed physiotherapy for her spine afterwards.

Just the ordeal of watching the ceremony was too much for the Duchess of Windsor when she spent three nights at the palace during the preparations for her husband's funeral in the summer of 1972. A memorable photograph was taken of her, looking sad and haggard, as she pulled aside a curtain at the palace window to watch the Queen's departure.

Trooping, which started in 1805, is in fact two events which come under the heading of the Queen's birthday parade. The intricate displays of Trooping the Colour and Mounting the Queen's Guard are performed on the Queen's 'official' birthday on the second Saturday in June. Each show of marching and counter marching is so complicated it cannot be written down and is passed by word of mouth from generation to generation.

In fact the origin of the two elements are obscure. Trooping the Colour probably began in the eighteenth century when battle colours were slowly carried along the lines so that soldiers, many of whom were foreign mercenaries, would remember which flag to rally round on the battlefield.

It was Prince Charles and Prince Philip who rallied to the Queen that fateful day in June 1981 when six shots, two spaced and the rest bunched, rang out from the crowd. Her son, in the uniform of the Welsh Guards, and husband, wearing the red and gold of the Grenadiers, trotted beside her as the Queen gentled Burmese.

She displayed the same poise and sangfroid which had earned Uncle David, Edward VIII, special tribute from the Archbishop of Canterbury following an attempt on his life during a colour ceremony. He was just returning to Buckingham Palace at the head of six battalions of Guards when, as the procession moved along Constitution

The Queen is the only woman to take part in the Trooping the Colour ceremony. Ironically it is held in June to avoid the wet British weather.

Hill, a loaded revolver was thrown a few feet from the King's horse by a demented Irish journalist.

Normally the only sound of gunfire is the 41-gun salute in Hyde Park which always makes the royal children jump as they watch the display of marching and counter marching on Horse Guards parade from the major-general's office. Princess Diana knows from experience that this complex series of well-defined drill movements cannot hold her boys enthralled for the full two hours. There are contingency plans. The royal handbag has a supply of sweets – soldiers are given barley sugars before the parade to help prevent fainting – and small plastic Action Man toys to relieve the tedium. Last year Prince Harry was so bored he flicked biscuits from the balcony on to the ranks of spectators below.

While the Trooping ceremony is world famous for its precision and timing – the Queen arrives at Horse Guards at eleven o'clock exactly – other horse-drawn royal events are not quite so perfectly organized. When the state coaches arrived outside one foreign embassy to pick up the white-tied ambassador and his counsellors to take them to Buckingham Palace for the time-honoured presentation of credentials, there was an unexpected hitch.

Just before the coaches, one containing the impressive personage of the Marshal of the Diplomatic Corps, made their dignified halt, a motorist parked outside the embassy. He refused to move until a Foreign Office official who oversees these occasions, reimbursed him for the £3 ($5.40) he had slotted into the parking meter.

While consuls are suitably conveyed in a royal coach, their wives, like so many coiffured Cinderellas, must travel behind the procession in a mere chauffeur-driven limousine. The reason is abstruse. In the last reign the Sovereign saw ambassadors who arrived by coach, in the morning, while his Queen Consort met their wives, who came by car, in the afternoon. The ceremony has been combined for this reign but the mode of transport has not changed.

At Buckingham Palace the convoy draws up outside the Grand Entrance where the diplomats alight, in some cases thankfully as these coaches are lightly sprung and have a rocking action. They are met by the Vice-Marshal of the Diplomatic Corps and the equerry before being ushered into the Bow Room for the summons to see the Queen who is waiting in the 1844 Room. French speakers are surprised by her linguistic ability, others are taken aback by her intimate knowledge of their country. 'As I was saying to your President . . .' is a phrase regularly dropped into the conversation after the envoy has presented the embossed leather-bound folder containing his personal credentials as well as a résumé of that nation's relations with Britain.

The Queen's long experience shows. When a South African ambassador presented his credentials, the Queen asked if there were still any films stored in the archives relating to her famous 1947 tour, where she nursed the secret of her romance with the future Duke of Edinburgh. 'My mother would so like to see them,' she remarked. As a result the Queen Mother was invited to the ambassador's penthouse flat over Trafalgar Square to see an old newsreel of the visit. 'Such a lovely exercise in nostalgia,' she recalled.

That kind of easy exchange, formality slipping into friendly conversation, would never have occurred in George VI's day. The King, who never truly conquered a life-long stutter, had little small talk and ambassadors were primed beforehand to start the dialogue. Things livened up considerably when an African envoy insisted on dancing and shaking after the King gave him a signed photograph in a silver frame.

Like her father, the Queen has maintained the tradition of ringing a silver bell to summon embassy counsellors but she has ended the bowing and walking out backwards which used to signify the end of a diplomatic audience. However this unseen royal theatre does serve its purpose of impressing those who have influence beyond Britain's shores. Diplomats are flattered by the display, respectful of the Sovereign's detailed grasp of events. It is hardly surprising. The monarchy has been running rather longer than *The Mousetrap* and the Queen knows her lines. When she fluffs, there is an under-secretary from the Foreign Office by her side ready to prompt. But that is a rare event.

When the Queen is abroad, her family smoothly slips into the part. During the Sovereign's absence two Counsellors of State take over her duties. Under present arrangements there are six – the Duke of Edinburgh, the Queen Mother, and her

The Queen, Prince Charles and Princess Diana travel to the Houses of Parliament.

The State Opening of Parliament is one of the most colourful constitutional ceremonies. The elaborate proceedings have been televised since 1958.

four children – who ·perform all the rituals of monarchy except that they are not able to dissolve Parliament, declare war and create peers.

The task of carrying out investitures is one which appeals to Prince Charles's sense of ceremonial and confirms Buckingham Palace's position as the fount of all honour. However this is one ceremony where the only sign of horses is the dismounted Household Cavalry who line each side of the Grand Staircase as the 300 recipients and their guests, who can still smell the lavender from the steward's brass burner, make their way to the cream and gold ballroom.

There are fourteen investitures each year at which the Queen or her representative lay their hands on 2,200 medals and decorations. The ceremony, which takes an hour and a half, demands unceasing concentration as twelve trayfuls of insignia are passed to the Queen, one at a time with never a hiccup. Even after she had three stitches in her hand when one of her corgis bit her, the Queen's behaviour was faultless. 'Corgis are horrible animals, she was very brave,' observed cricket commentator Brian Johnston sympathetically who couldn't help but notice the bandages as he received his CBE.

George VI's technique was so faultless that he could lay his hand on a medal without looking at it and often hummed along with the tunes being played by the string orchestra in the minstrels' gallery. 'For God's sake tell them not to make such a ghastly noise,' he would hiss to a courtier as the ranks of recipients awaited their moment of glory. The musicians too like to play their full part. They broke into a rendition of 'Limelight' when Charlie Chaplin was knighted and 'Bring Me Sunshine' for the comedy duo, Morecambe and Wise.

In fact the Queen still uses her father's Scots Guards sword when she gracefully taps the kneeling recipient on each shoulder with the flat of her sword. That is the theory. She likes to recall the time she knighted 'an enormous man'. 'I had to reach up with the sword. I heard a ripping noise and my sleeve got torn. It was hard to know who was the more embarrassed.'

The Queen never says 'Arise, sir knight' although the newly honoured shake her hand before backing away to take their seats. Knights are either nervous or nonchalant beforehand. 'My legs turned to jelly and the room swam before me,' recalled one soldier about to be decorated for bravery, while Sir Peter Ustinov was amused as much by the tangled protocol as the equally baffling explanation from a courtier.

The royal family itself is not immune to this stream of instruction explaining the minutiae of royal ceremonial. As Princess Diana adjusts the red poppy on the lapel of her black Valentino coat, she flicks through the three close-typed sheets which comprise supplementary notes for the annual Remembrance Day service at the Cenotaph in Whitehall. Every minute, every movement, from the greeting at 10.43 a.m. by the Home Secretary at the Quadrangle Door of the Foreign Office to the laying of wreaths at 11.02 a.m. after the Last Post has sounded, is laid down for the benefit of the royal participants.

There is no such plethora of paperwork involved when the Imperial State Crown is secretly trans-

The Household Divisions are the monarch's personal bodyguard. Their standing orders state that they must be able to reach the Sovereign within 24 hours – wherever they are stationed in the world.

When foreign ambassadors arrive to present their credentials to the Queen they are impressed by the dignified way they are conveyed.

ferred from the Tower of London to the billiard room at Buckingham Palace prior to the State Opening of Parliament. This priceless regalia, known as the Queen's 'going-away hat' as she wore it after the Coronation, is transported across London by a convoy of unmarked cars. Caution is essential. The crown, which travels in Queen Alexandra's state coach from Buckingham Palace to the Palace of Westminster, has 2,800 diamonds and other precious stones, yet is not insured.

Indeed the State Opening of Parliament, which takes place in the first week of November, brings together those powerful emblems of monarchy, horsemanship and jewellery, for an impressive pageant. On the day of what Princess Margaret calls 'a big dressing', the job of the royal dresser takes on special significance. They are the only members of staff allowed access to the Chubb wall safes, containing tiaras, orders and other jewellery, which are found in each royal apartment.

In fact the Queen has a safe in each of her homes, her dresser carrying the battered leather jewel cases by her side during the journey from the palace to Balmoral for the summer break. This security is in contrast to Queen Alexandra's day.

She used to display her jewellery in the glass cases in her dressing room.

The Princess of Wales, who is as happy wearing fake jewellery as the real thing, finds these formal occasions tricky. While her cropped hairstyle is fine for her morning swim, it makes life difficult when she and her dresser try and ease on the Spencer tiara as she prepares for a State Opening of Parliament. One year she inadvertently incurred the Queen's displeasure by wearing her blonde hair in a bold chignon style to cope with her tiara. As might be expected the media concentrated on the new royal hair-do and not the content of the Queen's speech. The Sovereign was not amused.

There are occasions too when even the placid carriage horses behave badly. Princess Anne recalled how she had to get out of her carriage when something startled the horses outside Clarence House. She told Sue MacGregor, 'One of them kicked over the traces and they turned round and faced the carriage and the whole thing came to a grinding halt in the middle of The Mall. We were dressed in just the sort of thing you wear on a mid-November morning in London, like a long white dress, tiara and uniform. In terms of classic occasions for breaking down in the wrong place at the wrong time that probably took the biscuit.'

The Queen has her own problems as she attempts to balance a crown weighing three pounds and which always gives her neckache whilst trying to read a speech, written by the prime minister, which outlines the legislative programme in the forthcoming session of Parliament. Her grandfather George V had the speech typed on thick parchment so that the assembled peers and commoners would not notice his hands trembling, while Edward VIII found the smell of mothballs from the colourful robes and ermine 'suffocating'.

Little wonder that the Queen and her party return to Buckingham Palace with a feeling of relief. 'Minded the store well, Chips?' she used to say to the Lord Chamberlain who remains at the palace as a 'hostage' for the Sovereign's safe return. For the store, this hodgepodge of office, museum and high-class theatre, is still the family home of the Firm. It is the place where the 'high-pitched girlish voices' of the royal family are heard chattering in the Picture Gallery and where gener-

ations of excited royal children have marvelled at the RAF flypast at the end of the birthday parade, blithely playing amidst the precious porcelain.

'That looks lovely, mummy,' Prince William tells his mother as she does a twirl in her jewels and silks before heading off for a banquet or dressy reception at Buckingham Palace. Endless entertainment and the celebration of ceremonial are as much a part of life in this royal village as the liveried footmen and patrolling policemen.

However the palace is far more than a grander version of a Disneyland spectacular. Buckingham Palace is the headquarters of a working monarchy which effortlessly and energetically exercises its authority, ensuring that the entire body politic and civic is swept into its embrace. The palace is the powerhouse for a revitalized European monarchy and ranks alongside the White House and the Kremlin as an institution which has international recognition.

At the same time the palace has a unique potency which extends far beyond its wrought-iron gates. The deep-rooted and powerful mystique which monarchy exerts on the popular imagination is symbolized by the palace. It is the shrine to our hopes, celebrations, sorrows and, ultimately, our dreams. Buckingham Palace has truly earned its position as an enduring emblem at the centre of our national life.

The Changing of the Guard ceremony is a popular tourist attraction. Now, soldiers are often armed.

APPENDIX
The Cost of Running Buckingham Palace

Good housekeeping is a watchword at the palace, the Queen setting an example by turning off lights, reducing heating and introducing computers to monitor expenditure. 'If you are cold, put on a sweater,' is an oft-used royal phrase but this has not stopped an increase in spending of about 40 per cent since 1983. It now costs around £1.6 ($2.8) million a year simply to run Buckingham Palace, with general maintenance – paid for by the Department of the Environment – and staff salaries on top.

Palace pay is poor, the total wage bill for the approximately 330 staff amounting to under £3 ($5.4) million a year. Around 80 per cent of the staff earn under £10,000 ($18,000) a year, with an average salary of around £160 ($288) a week. In fairness, live-in staff receive free board and lodging. Housemaids earn around £4,300 ($7,740), senior footmen about £8,000 ($14,400) and information officers and clerks between £12,000 ($21,600) and £14,000 ($26,320). Highest paid is the Queen's private secretary Sir Robert Fellowes who earns £60,000 ($108,000) a year.

The spiralling burden of security is demonstrated by the fact that in 1991 the deputy assistant metropolitan commissioner John Cracknell in charge of royal and diplomatic protection earned more than the private secretary with a salary of £61,000 ($110,000). While total spending on the Civil List and the royal family was expected to be around £56 ($100.8) million for the year 1990–91, this excludes security which is now the largest single item of expenditure.

In London alone the Metropolitan Police spent £50 ($90) million on royal and diplomatic protection while Thames Valley police have recruited extra uniformed officers to guard the Duke and Duchess of York's new home. Police authorities monitoring the Queen's private homes of Balmoral and Sandringham regularly request additional funds and manpower. It means that the cost of policing royal events, palaces and private homes far exceeds expenditure on the monarchy. The cost of running Buckingham Palace is shown below.

	1983		1990 estimate	
	£	$	£	$
Domestic Expenses				
Royal kitchens	158,463	285,233	200,783	361,409
Royal cellars	24,588	44,258	71,250	128,250
Furnishings	123,183	221,729	180,558	325,004
Laundry	27,986	50,374	63,700	114,660
Flowers	37,838	68,108	37,950	68,310
Livery	45,732	82,317	88,100	158,580
Garden parties	149,986	269,974	213,650	384,570
Horses and Carriages				
Purchase	3,162	5,691	16,000	28,800
Upkeep and repairs	118,867	213,948	149,025	268,245
Motor Cars				
Purchase and hire	25,865	46,557	37,042	66,675
Upkeep and repairs	42,802	77,043	36,275	65,295

£1 = $1.80

Source: Royal Trustees/Metropolitan Police

	1983		1990 estimate	
	£	$	£	$
Office Expenses				
Equipment	75,801	136,441	123,150	221,670
Stationery	173,925	313,065	138,900	250,020
Newspapers	7,459	13,426	13,532	24,395
Insurance	13,652	24,573	29,000	52,200
Travel	33,027	59,448	50,840	91,512
Official presents	6,984	12,571	34,000	61,200
Donations and prizes	4,728	8,510	9,500	17,100
Gratuities	27,130	48,834	30,933	55,679
Sundry expenses	60,680	109,224	88,630	159,534
TOTAL	1,161,858	2,091,344	1,601,817	2,883,270

Related Government Expenditure

	1983		1990 estimate	
Upkeep of Buckingham Palace and other royal residences	10.678m	19.22m	25.65m	46.17m
Equerries	69,000	124,200	192,000	345,600
Marshal of the Diplomatic Service	21,546	38,782	53,807	96,852
Gentlemen-at-arms/ Yeoman of the Guard	29,000	52,200	48,000	86,400